The Curves of Time
the memoirs of
Oscar Niemeyer

I am not attracted to straight angles or to the straight line, hard and inflexible, created by man. I am attracted to free-flowing, sensual curves. The curves that I find in the mountains of my country, in the sinuousness of its rivers, in the waves of the ocean, and on the body of the beloved woman. Curves make up the entire Universe, the curved Universe of Einstein.

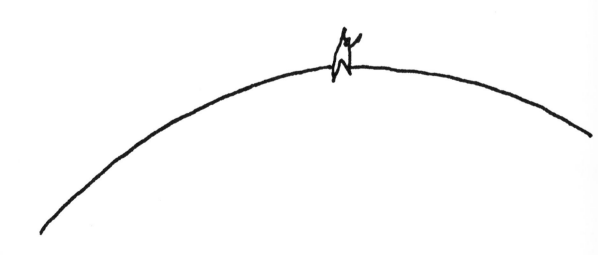

Phaidon Press Limited
Regent's Wharf
All Saints Street
London N1 9PA

First published in English 2000
© 2000 Phaidon Press Limited
First published in Portuguese by Editora Revan

Translated from the Portuguese by Izabel Murat Burbridge

ISBN 0 7148 4007 6

A CIP catalogue record for this book is available from the British Library.

Designed by Sam Blok
Printed in China

Illustration Credits: All photographs and sketches courtesy Oscar Niemeyer Foundation,
Rio de Janeiro, except the following: p. 116, pp. 151–58 © Wayne Andrews/Esto

On re-reading this book, I feel that it uncovers two distinct personas. One looks on the bright side of life and sees the fun part of it that has always attracted me. The other has a pessimistic view of life and society in general, and is angered by the injustices of this world.

Both personas were profoundly influenced by architecture as an inner calling, heeded so passionately that it has engaged them both for an entire lifetime.

This explains the alternating instances of euphoria and unease that have permeated my mediocre life. It was in relation to my friendships that these mood swings were most intense and heartfelt.

I have always cherished my friends and nurtured our friendships. I took great pleasure from taking them along on visits to the Old World. What a joy it was to see some of them enjoying things they had never imagined possible!

Then there was my family. . . I have always loved them so! Whenever I thought of them, from afar, I felt so moved, and when I was near them, oh how I loved them! For them, I did my best and gave my all.

That is the way I have lived my life.

I have never been one to look back and regret mistakes. I am a child of Nature, a tiny and insignificant part of her, and in her lies the credit or the blame–partly, at any rate–for both my qualities and my faults. This is the way she made me.

O.N.

Saturdays and Sundays are the days when I get through the most work at my office on Avenida Atlantica. I sit alone and browse through books, take up some writing, draw, think about life, or just look out on the beautiful ocean at Copacabana Beach.

They say that Descartes stayed in bed until 11:00 A.M. dreaming up his theories, and this is what I try to do on days when most people relax on the beach or watch a soccer game. During this apparent lull, I get to know myself better as I indulge in a kind of self-criticism that does me a world of good.

Today is Saturday. During one such idle moment I figured I could write a book about my life and issues as an architect in this fleeting passage that fate affords us. This book would set out my views and point out the innermost feelings that have influenced this insignificant existence of mine as a human being. I would write of my concern for the matters of life and of this fantastic universe we inhabit as uninvited guests. The book would show how I have always sought to make time for the broader view, to feel indignation against injustice, exploitation, and the neglect of the underprivileged members of our society.

I would also write of my origins, my faults and virtues, my disbelief in the face of our paradoxical world, and my determination to join the most valiant fighters in an attempt to improve it a little. I would also talk of the hidden being lurking within, a creation of our genetic codes, that is partly responsible for our actions and attitudes. I would say that it is a lubricious and imaginative being that impels us toward sexuality, architectural creativity, and fantasy.

My dear friend Rodrigo M. F. de Andrade once gave me some advice: "Get on with the writing, you can polish it up afterward." So that is what I intend to do, dear reader; I shall be spontaneous and straightforward, and my easy flow of language will not tax your patience.

I shall start by remembering my origins. My name ought to be Oscar Ribeiro Soares or Oscar Ribeiro de Almeida de Niemeyer Soares, but the foreign name prevailed and I became known as Oscar Niemeyer. My ethnic roots are diverse, something I find particularly gratifying. Ribeiro and Soares are Portuguese names, Almeida is Arabic, and Niemeyer is German. Not to mention the blacks or Indians who, unknown to us, may also have been part of our family.

The houses we live in leave some of the most lasting impressions on us: the atmosphere of our family life, the issues we take on throughout our lifetime. Behind those old walls that separated us from the world outside, the family grew up, and we lived through joys and sorrows as the years went by so unrelentingly.

The yearning to go back again and relive those bygone times brings to mind the old houses that have sheltered me from youth through old age. Some have vanished, a few are still there, and many have been worn down–like myself–by the passing years: walls drooping, floors sagging, roofs pierced by the inevitable leakages.

From memory, I will revisit my childhood home in the district of Laranjeiras. I will walk through it again, remembering just how we inhabited it, laughing or crying, as we lived our destiny.

I was born and raised in that house. I married Annita in that house, and that is where our daughter, Anna Maria, was also born. It was a two-story house with six front windows and a frontispiece inscribed with the letters "RA," the initials of my grandfather's surname, Ribeiro de Almeida. The ground floor held the entrance hall, studio, living room, dining room, the bedrooms of my Uncle Nhonhô and Aunt Ziza, my grandparents' suite, bathrooms, dinette, kitchen, backyard, and the servants' quarters. On the upper floor were my parents' suite, cousin Milota's bedroom, the bedrooms of my sisters Lilia, Leonor, and Judith, and our bedrooms– those of my brothers Carlos Augusto and Paulo, and mine.

What feelings of nostalgia that house brings to mind! The heavenly peace in which we lived, the large dining table around which the whole family gathered: my grandmother at the head, my grandfather, aunt, and uncle on one side; and my parents, brothers and sisters, cousin Milota, and myself on the other.

We children didn't talk at the table; we just listened to the conversation of our elders. As soon as we had finished eating, I would run outside. Whenever the front gate was shut, I would jump over the iron fence at the point where we had cut off its spiked tips.

After dinner the family gathered on the veranda. Sometimes Aunt Maria Eugênia, who lived down the street, came over with her husband, Nelson Cavalcanti, a medical doctor whose story-telling and amusing laugh livened up the conversation. And it was in this pleasurable environment that my family drew the plans that all families nurture, but life implacably interrupts.

My grandfather had a sole concern: not to become a burden to anyone. I remember my grandmother scolding me every time I went out to skate on the veranda. "Won't you stop that? You're disturbing your grandfather!" she would say. But in no time he would show up at the window and announce: "Skate all you want, you won't bother me."

But this arbitrary attitude that my grandmother undoubtedly brought with her from her farm in Maricá, and which by no means prevented her from being a top-notch housewife, manifested itself now and then in her outbursts: "Take that cloth off your head. Colored folk don't wear such things." Even though I was only six or seven years old, the way she talked to the housemaid particularly upset me. My grandmother was religious, as was our whole family. Mass was held regularly at our house, with family members and our neighbors in attendance. On those days, she opened one of the five windows in the sitting room—its windowsill served as oratory—and recited the "Hail Mary" out loud. At times, when she was in one of her particularly insolent moods, my grandfather would say, very gently, "Heaven help us, that's one bossy woman." But they were always great friends. I remember him, in his old age, sitting in the studio and eating his lunch, with my grandmother keeping him company and pampering him, forever concerned about his health.

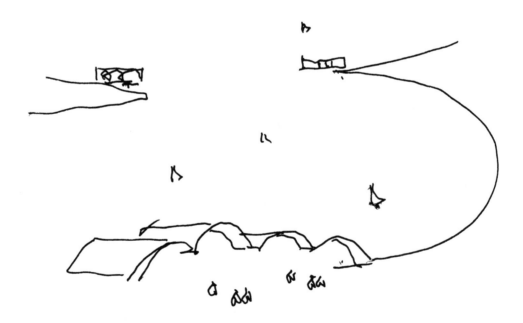

The family always received a great many guests. On such days, our manservant, André, served dinner at small tables set out on the veranda. After dinner, the party retired to the sitting room where someone played the piano, my mother sang, and our cousin Heloísa belted out her favorite aria from *Rigoletto*. These were little gatherings typical of those days, attended only by family members and close friends, and definitely quite dull.

Illustrious people paid frequent visits to our house, people such as Brazil's former President Epitácio Pessoa,[2] and Minister of State André Cavalcanti, my grandfather's professional colleague. "Counselor," the latter said to him one day, "don't ever retire. The grass will grow high around your doorstep."

My grandfather was intrinsically honest, and, having occupied important positions such as Attorney General of the Republic and Minister of the Federal Supreme Court, he died poor, leaving only that house in Laranjeiras as a legacy to his four children. This example was always very important to me.

One day, as I looked out of the window (I was only seven years old then), I saw the street atypically filled with cars and people carrying a coffin out through our front gate. I didn't understand what was going on, or that I would never see my grandfather again.

I remember teasing my Grandmother Mariquinhas for locking up all the doors and windows every night with a bunch of keys she carried at her waist. And if I criticized her, may the dear old lady forgive me–she and our friend Tristão de Athayde[3] who, in an article published in the *Jornal do Brasil* newspaper in which he praised my unpretentious language, described her as a wonderful individual, an old friend of his family.

I don't know if you've ever heard it said that marriages among relatives don't work, and this may explain the unique figures of my Uncle Nhonhô and my Aunt Ziza, born out of my grandfather's marriage to one of his nieces.

Antônio Augusto Ribeiro de Almeida, Son (as he signed his letters), was my Uncle Nhonhô's full name. How I loved this uncle! His carefree attitude toward life, his inventive spirit, always trying to do everything differently. Sometimes I peered through the library door and there was Nhonhô lying on the sofa, undoubtedly thinking of other things, while the priest, his private tutor from law school, impassively drilled the day's lesson. My grandmother allowed him to indulge all his fantasies; with money in his pocket, Nhonhô had an "easy and miraculous" lifestyle, like that of old Bocage's.[4]

As a boy, he at times hired a taxi to take his friends and himself, sticks in hand, to fight with the boys who lived on neighboring streets. As a grown man, he went on fighting in the soccer fields and bars of Rio de Janeiro. One day, so great was the ruckus at Bar Americano in the Cruzeiro shopping arcade, that not one picture was left hanging on its walls. At Nhonhô's request I reproduced the scene in a large gouache painting whose authorship I always concealed from my friends. I have always looked at it out of the corner of my eye, feeling guilty for having created such a terrible painting.

After he married, my uncle decided to leave the city. He bought a small property in Jacarepaguá, used the wood from the bower at our house to build a small cottage, and, accompanied by Eleonora, his wife, settled there under the trees, not giving a damn about the world, just like Robinson Crusoe. He wrote short stories as a pastime, and even had a book published: *Grãos que alimentam o mundo* (Grains that Feed the World).

Sometimes we went down to see him, and we always got a laugh right at the entrance. Instead of a doorbell, he had a light switch that announced the visitor's arrival by turning off the radio that was always blasting away inside the house. Nhonhô would come out to greet us, swinging his arms and smiling happily. Then we would sit and visit outside the house, which was so small that really only he and his wife fit in it.

"Look, I'm going to put in a little addition here. It'll be great," he would say. Invariably we turned to look sympathetically at his wife, who once had led the standard sheltered life of the Brazilian upper classes, accustomed to all possible amenities, and was now sharing my uncle's fantasies. He often took me to the local bar for a beer. Stopping at the gate, he called out to his eleven dogs, "You, you, and you can come along," and those selected three dogs would follow us and wait while we drank. Finally, my uncle's friends would escort us to the bar door and the dogs would follow us back home. How I loved this uncle of mine! One day he got sick and my brother Paulo took him to the hospital, Casa de Saúde Eiras. That same afternoon I went to visit him. I found him sitting up in bed, submissively declaiming one of his favorite mottos: "You can't fight nature."

A month after his death, with the dogs lying meekly under the trees, neighborhood friends realized that everything was far too quiet at the couple's home. When they went into the house, they found the body of my uncle's wife, who possibly had died because she wished to follow him as she had done all her life. "Men go wherever is convenient to them, and women accompany their husbands," my grandfather Ribeiro de Almeida used to say in those rare moments when he played a macho role.

I had just been speaking of our house in the Laranjeiras neighborhood of Rio, when in [to my studio] walked my cousin Camargo carrying four old wall tiles. Once he had left and I was alone, I looked at those tiles on my desk, at their blue patterns on a white background, and felt sentimental. How they brought back memories! Such nostalgia for times gone forever. They came from the veranda wall fronting the living rooms and my grandparents' bedrooms. Those tiles listened in on so many conversations; they looked on as we held parties with the tables pushed back against the tiled walls, and André served guests with the humility that the ruling classes have always favored in their servants.

I fingered the tiles slowly and thought of Henry Miller running his hand on the top of Balzac's desk and wondering, like me, what it could tell of the great genius that had spent a lifetime huddled over it. What secrets are stored in those tiles under the apparent inertia of fired clay! I fell into a melancholy contemplation of those four lone tiles scattered on the desk. Then I carefully collected them. This is all that remains of the years we lived in that house in Laranjeiras.

I open an old family album and a picture of Milota draws my attention. She looks so sad, so embittered, that I stop a bit to think: Could our cousin really have been as unhappy as she looks in this photo? And I look on, moved by memories of how good she was to me all my life. In my earliest recollections she was already old and fat, fanning herself and leaning on a cane to walk around the house. And if on the one hand I gave her a lot of trouble, if sometimes I failed to grant her the attention and care she so deserved, on the other hand I was the child she had never had, and thus I served, to some extent, to fill her empty, spinsterly life. I came to her with all sorts of requests. Upon arriving home from school, I would go straight to her bedroom before going out to play, munching on a bread-and-chocolate sandwich she would have waiting for me. At dinnertime, while I ate she quietly mashed up avocado with sugar and lemon juice for my dessert, or discreetly passed me sweets under the table, making sure no one else would notice.

For twenty years we lived in that house in Laranjeiras. Later, however, after my grandfather's death, we decided to make our life simpler. My father, my sisters, and my brother Paulo went to live in Ipanema. I moved with Annita, Anna Maria, and Milota to a row house on a dead-end alley off Rua Visconde de Pirajá.

Naturally, I am still filled with an enormous sense of loss when I think of Milota, but it comforts me to feel that together we lived through some of the happiest moments of our lives.

Milota was removed from the world and from mundane things. One day in 1945, Luís Carlos Prestes,[5] leader of the Brazilian Communist Party, phoned me. Startled at hearing his name, she asked, "Didn't they say this man was crazy?" Poor Milota! She merely repeated what she heard from the contemporary bourgeoisie, totally unaware of the more equitable world that Prestes, courageous man that he was, desired.

My parents were such wonderful people. I never knew them to quarrel or heard their voices raised in anger. They lived for each other and both of them were entirely devoted to us children. Their

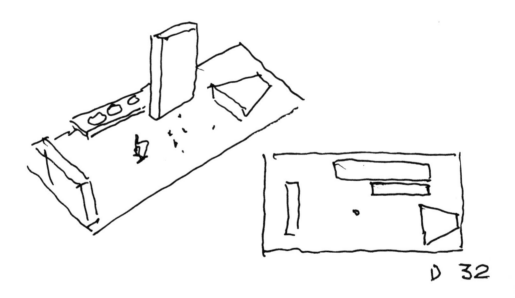

lives were so pleasant, so uncomplicated, and so humdrum that I can think of nothing special to relate.

I am gazing at old family snapshots again, curious to see how we looked so many years ago, and how we have withstood the passing of time and the tricks of life, with its unexpected and inevitable mishaps.

Now I am holding a photo of my mother, still young, surely engaged to be married. At her side is my father with his forelocks and boots, wearing a stiff shirtfront and ascot. A friend of my mother, Leonor Aragão, is also seated, and my aunts Ziza and Maria Eugênia are standing behind them. My mother looks pretty and earnest, her hair swept into a bun, and she is wearing a slender-waisted high-necked dress in the fashion of the day.

I dig out more photos and find one of her with my father, apparently now married. He has a mustache, and she is wearing a plain dress and has that air of serenity that has always been one of her qualities.

More photos: here is one taken twenty years later. We are in the garden at our house in Laranjeiras; my mother and father are standing with Lilia, Carlos Augusto, and Leonor. Judith, Paulo, and I are sitting in front of them. My mother has put on weight and my father is losing his hair, but the family scene exudes sheer happiness.

Still more photos. Mother no longer has the same cheerful and relaxed countenance, and I sense a hint of sadness. Perhaps this was the illness she was hiding from us; a few months later it took her away forever. After that date, all the photos of my father are more recent, as if something had prevented him from being photographed during a long period of recovery.

There are more photos with children and grandchildren, and photos taken at my Copacabana studio. I am struck by the fact that five or six photos like these can cover an entire lifetime's adventure of two people falling in love, having children, growing old, experiencing their share of happiness and misfortune, and then both vanishing from this earth. . . forever.

Occasionally I have to break off from my writing to answer the phone or recall something that strikes me or especially moves me. My little book will surely be more up-to-date on account of this intertwining of past and present and, who knows, perhaps even a little more readable.

Today, for instance, I have come to the office but have no appetite for writing. I am not sure why, perhaps because the dull weather is bothering me; the ocean and the sky meld in a cheerless hue of gray. I wonder what it is that has affected me so. My mind travels far back to those troubled times that we all have at one period or another.

Bitter memories come to mind against my will: relatives and friends who have passed away, minor offenses magnified by the passing of time. I used to think that I could make up for them at some point, but I was wrong. Fortunately, there was no grave misdemeanor, rather a lack of consideration for those who preceded me and passed on to the void beyond. I feel the urge to go back in time and embrace them warmly. Such a poignant feeling. *Navegar é preciso* (To sail is a need).[6] Yet there are many people who depend on me, and architecture beckons with fresh challenges.

I wander out to the balcony to distract myself and watch the ocean pounding on the beach, so deserted it seems that a huge wave of desolation has engulfed everyone.

My mind turns to my dear comrades of the Brazilian Communist Party, the PCB, and I can hear their voices echoing, "Away with pessimism, Oscar. This world is a wonderful place and our task is to make it even more joyful and happy." I have to agree with them; despite all the suffering, this life is so full of beauty that we must cherish it and have eyes only for the flowers scattered across this rock-strewn terrain.

I hear a knock on the door; a few friends drop by. Estelita yells for ice, Rômulo[7] has brought along a couple of bottles of something. They are followed by Renato Guimarães, Sabino Barroso, Ivan Alves, Fernando Balbi, and Carlos Niemeyer.[8] They are often joined by João Saldanha, Glauco Campelo, Montenegro,[9] and others. Estelita loves to recall names and dates from the past, remembering our good old times at Sacha's and Night and Day.[10] Rômulo, who describes himself as a progressive socialist while quoting Roberto Campos,[11] harks back to his exploits in Rio and Recife. Renato is more instructive and has a penchant for righting past political wrongs, while João Saldanha ranges from soccer lore and his world travels to the yarns of an old Communist Party activist. Ivan is a pleasant and agreeable fellow; if anyone should ask, "Who played for Flamengo in 1930?" he's always ready to reel off the soccer team's lineup. Carlos Niemeyer is unfailingly cheerful and keeps our spirits up. How these little get-togethers do wonders for me!

I am a straightforward person. I take an interest in life in all its forms and am open to all the changes that new times may bring. That is why I can understand why our family developed the way it did, why the sad but inevitable generation gap grew as young people demanded the freedom to forge their own future. I nevertheless recall the past with fond nostalgia, while, of course, not forgetting its negative side.

There was the inward-looking family circle, sometimes generous to the less privileged, but always ready to hold on to its own favors and privileges as the first priority. Parents did the talking and children respectfully obeyed them. But there was a lifelong bond of friendship between them, as if together they made up a single and indestructible whole. Such was home life with my parents and brothers and sisters. Even today, after so many years, we are very close. . . and do we stick up for each other! We certainly nurture that longstanding and undying bond of friendship.

There were six of us siblings: Lilia, Carlos Augusto, Leonor, Judite, Paulo, and myself. Carlos Augusto and Judite have passed away. Lilia is married to musician João Nunes and has a son, two daughters, and three grandchildren. Leonor has remained single. Paulo married Marisa and has nine children and five grandchildren. I am married to Annita and have a daughter, four grandchildren, and seven great-grandchildren.

My first school was on Rua Soares Cabral and the headmistress was Dona Hermínia Lyra da Silva. It was a small, semidetached, one-story house with a garden on one side.

I recall walking to school with our housemaid along Rua das Laranjeiras, carrying my schoolbag. One day my mother told us to walk on the opposite sidewalk because it was said that somebody who lived on our side of the street had come down with diphtheria; such was the fear of infection that her concern was only reasonable.

My only recollections of those times are of my drawings of coffee pots, cups, and figurines, and of always getting top marks for them. My mother proudly kept them, not realizing that they someday would lead me on to architecture.

After schooling with Dona Hermínia, I attended the Barnabite fathers' school on Rua do Catete. This was an excellent school with a fine tradition of instruction, although it had its good and bad teachers like anywhere else. I remember that I was top of the class in my first year there and Olavo Bahia was second; the following year he was first and I was second. But after that I lost interest in everything except soccer and dropped to the bottom of the class.

There were three soccer fields at the school and I was so crazy about the game that Horácio Werne, the history teacher, banned me from the field for two or three days as punishment. I guess I was quite a good player. I recall that some time later Amado Benigno, the great Flamengo goalkeeper and a friend of mine, asked me to turn out with his team.

There was no class on Thursdays, so on Wednesday evenings I met up with schoolmates and a whole bunch of us would go downtown to ogle the ladies. One day my uncle clued me in: "The Lapa district is not right for you; come by my office on Thursday." He took me to a downtown rendezvous and sat me down at a table. A woman came up and said: "So what do you think you're doing here, my boy?"

I caught a dose of gonorrhea and the doctor prescribed methyl blue, so I was able to impress my classmates by magically peeing blue urine.

One day, some red blotches appeared on my hand and with a frightened voice I asked Father Victor, the assistant dean, if I could go home. He shouted angrily that it was just paint. Since I paid no heed he added, "Go home then, and don't come back until your father has had a talk with me."

It was indeed paint. But I never did go back to that school. Instead, I finished my schooling at another school, the French Lyceum.

Between leaving the French Lyceum and enrolling at the School of Fine Arts, my life was eventful but mostly trouble-free and full of leisure. From the age of seventeen until I married at twenty-one I lived a carefree life; it seemed that time had stood still for a while so that I could play around a little. I remember staying out on the town one night, and the next morning mother and father were posted at the gate anxiously awaiting my return. "Let me be the one to scold him!" my mother pleaded. But then she ran up and only hugged me. Afterward, she told my old man how she had been at a loss for words from being so overjoyed that I was back.

When not at the Café Lamas, the Fluminense Futebol Clube or the Clube de Regatas Guanabara, I was to be found in Lapa, then a famed red-light district symbolized by the madam Laurinha Tinguassu.[12]

This recollection brings to mind old friends now gone forever: Antônio Jacobina, João Brandão, Horácio de Carvalho, Silvio

Cavalcanti, Alfredo and Casimiro Rodrigues, Tico Liberal, Oyama Rios¹⁵. . . What fond memories of that halcyon youth of friendships and shared visions of the future!

Café Lamas was our cafeteria-cum-office, our daily meeting place and starting point for nighttime adventures. There we talked, played pool, and laughed the night away.

Sometimes we would go to the movie theater on Avenida Rio Branco. Live musicians played along with the movies, among them a rather elderly violinist. It used to bother me that an old man was obliged to perform such exertions just for our entertainment. Or we would go straight to the Lapa and wander around the bars, chatting with and embracing the women we met there until the night inevitably drew to its orgiastic finale.

Sunday was our day for a soccer game. . . or maybe the Politeama movie theater. Oyama would rush over to the pianist and ask him to play the aria "Cuore Ingrato" (Ungrateful Heart) as the "soundtrack," so we could joke and amuse ourselves watching "heroic" movies starring Tom Mix or William Hart.¹⁴

For a long time, I was a regular at a recreational club called Clube de Regatas Guanabara. Many an evening was spent in fondly remembered samba sessions with Siri Buceta (Crab the Cunt), Micarema the Boatman, and Dog's Life Gastão, a young and jobless

guitarist who practically lived at the club, day and night, playing his favorite samba:

Where's that money I gave you
To keep for me, you son of a bitch
That money I gave you
You spent it, son of a bitch

He and the rest of them were all good people, however, and I will never forget them.

Occasionally, a bunch of us from the club, including Serpa, who played on the Brazilian waterpolo team, would go dancing at samba school arenas or at the Caprichosos da Estopa dancehall in Botafogo. The mulatto women were beautiful and Serpa's brother, who was the master of ceremonies and ensured the family atmosphere of the venue, always greeted us proudly.

We were fascinated by Rio's nightlife, in which we made our début at the Políticos cabaret on Rua do Passeio, though we were often barred from entry for being underage. We loved its party environment, the pretty women, the wildly changing fortunes of roulette and baccarat.

Afterward, we would walk along the streets back to Laranjeiras, regretfully saying goodbye as friends reached their doors. Our earnestly protracted conversations seemed more intimate and fraternal in the silence of the night, on the slumbering city streets, as if life were fair for one and all.

In 1928, I married Annita Baldo, the pretty daughter of Italian immigrants originally from Padua, near Venice. At the time I had no clear idea of what I wanted to do with myself. On the contrary, I was leading the nonchalant life of a bohemian, without a care in the world. But once married I began to realize the responsibility I had assumed, and I went to work at my father's typesetting business before enrolling in the National School of Fine Arts.

I recall the early days of our marriage, when Annita helped me with school projects and I was always divided between architecture and typesetting.

My daughter Anna Maria was born. My mother underwent surgery and was taken to recover at a house on Avenida Atlântica, in Copacabana, with my father and my sisters. We were short of money and now, without my parents and sisters, the Laranjeiras house seemed too big for us. There was an atmosphere of decadence and neglect in its empty rooms. It was only after the deaths of my aunt and my grandmother that we decided to make things easier by moving out. My parents and sisters remained in Copacabana while I rented a small house in Leblon for my wife and myself, my daughter Anna Maria, and my cousin Milota.

It was a small two-bedroom house. Milota slept in one bedroom and Anna Maria in the other. My wife and I slept on a folding sofa bed in the living room with a veranda opening onto a small garden. The house was simple, friendly, and quiet. We practically lived off the rent from a house owned by Milota. We ate at a boarding house and we had no housemaid, but the whole world seemed to smile on us.

Our needs were minimal in comparison to the normal standards of consumer society. We had no icebox or household appliances. We did not even own a car. Our only indulgence was the occasional pair of new shoes, a shirt, or a dress. We were young and happy, optimistic about life and the world.

On Sundays we visited with my father and then stayed home at night, happily chatting to whoever was around: Hélio Uchôa, Milton Roberto, José Reis, or our friend and neighbor Paulo Werneck.[15]

As time passed, I met with some professional success and built a house on Rua Carvalho de Azevedo, and later another one on Estrada das Canoas. But those times of hardship at the little house in Leblon always brought back our fondest memories. "It was so much better!" Annita used to say for many years afterward.

We often went to the Botanical Gardens, where I loved to walk along the gravel paths and admire the lush tropical vegetation, or pause by plants to read the complicated scientific names, or look at the pond and the huge water lilies and everlastings blooming everywhere. Every so often I stopped to draw a plant, attempting to capture it with a few strokes of my architectural perspective.

Annita followed along happily, and Anna Maria cheerfully ran ahead of us. Sometimes it was the imperial palms that caught my attention with their tall, elegant, and stately trunks reaching skyward. Or I was struck by the unusual shape of an exotic plant I hadn't seen before.

Nature is so beautiful! How it multiplies everywhere and maintains structural logic in all its secrets!

Few people walked around the Botanical Gardens as much as we did, or were as doggedly curious as we were. We used to get there early, at about 11:00 A.M., as the golden light filtered through the branches of the enormous trees and left shadowed patterns on the ground. We ecstatically sensed the perfection of Nature, when Man treats it with respect. It would be so wonderful if we could preserve the spontaneity that is so often sacrificed when those supposedly responsible for protecting nature do not understand it!

Oh, the old gardens of Rio! The Passeio Público, Campo de Santana, and Floresta da Tijuca, all of them beautifully laid out by Don João VI,[16] who imported special seedlings that eventually took root here, producing trees that today are part of our extraordinary flora. How welcoming are the graveled paths of Tijuca, shaded by the tropical vegetation! Occasional small details enhance these paths through their exaggerated contrast with the exuberant vegetation.

Just look at what has happened to all the fruit-bearing trees of my childhood years! Banana, mango, jaboticaba, avocado trees. . .all uprooted and replaced by streets jammed with vehicles and expressways with concrete parapets. Yet I mean no criticism of our landscape designers, with their excellent professional approach and understanding, who were influenced by the terraced gardens of the Portuguese tradition and by the Japanese school, which is based on allowing Nature to grow freely, as if untouched by human hand.

I have long been thinking of one day paying a visit to the Botanical Gardens to relive the same rapture of forty or fifty years ago.

After listening to the tapes recorded for this book I have concluded that all this talk of family members, one after the other, will bore my readers. So let me tell you I just had a conversation with Darcy Ribeiro[17] and he was so excited over the forthcoming inauguration of the Sambódromo [a stadium built for carnival parades] and the Centros Integrados de Educaçao Pública (Integrated Centers of Public Education), or CIEPs.[18] And my dear old friend was right to feel so excited, because these two projects have triumphed against all odds after a whole bunch of lies were invented in an attempt to snuff them out. First it was said that the Sambódromo would not be built on time. Then, word went around that there were engineering problems with a river channel under the stands that would overflow with heavy rains. Even St. Peter [patron saint of weather] was dragged into the fray!

But none of the threatened scenarios actually materialized. José Carlos Sussekind's[19] architectural work was flawless. There were no floods, no problems with the river—which turned out to be just a creek—and the job was beautifully finished on time, within the schedule set by Brizola[20] and Darcy.

So now we have the Sambódromo, all ready to receive 120,000 spectators; we have the Apoteose Plaza, the area for the concluding climax of the parade (this was Darcy Ribeiro's idea), which rounds out the composition with a beautiful concrete curve. One feature that was not publicized at the time—because it would have meant praising Darcy Ribeiro—was his idea of having classrooms built under the venue's bleachers and boxes. A stadium-school for 15,000 pupils! France's Minister of Culture Jack Lang[21] enthused, "I have never seen anything like this!"

What about the new CIEPs schools program? The opposition [to the Brizola state government] cannot stomach having to see these new schools springing up everywhere! Suspended from their concrete supports and brightly painted, they certainly stand out from the surrounding buildings, as we intended them to. They provide an entirely new kind of education that involves not just schooling but also keeping the kids off the streets—with meals, study periods, and sports, all good preparation for the hard life ahead of these students.

Darcy is bearing a confident smile of satisfaction at seeing a job well done. I have known him for a long time, since the days when he alone struggled to have a new university built in Brasília, and this dear companion had as much enthusiasm and success then as he has today. Darcy eventually got involved in politics, and was appointed minister of education and head of President João Goulart's office. In fact, he was the last man out of the presidential building when the coup took place in 1964. He is not only the intelligent and creative person known to all, but also a loyal friend through thick and thin.

After Darcy left the room I remained gazing at the shelf with the many books he published which put Brazilian intelligence and culture on display for the whole world to see.

We always admire people who are what we ourselves would like to be, so my brother Carlos Augusto was a model for me. I was so fond of him! Always easygoing, always taking an interest in things, even in passing concerns, and carefully guarding his own bitter disappointments; it seemed he avoided mentioning them so as not to upset us.

Carlos Augusto began his professional career at the age of seventeen, at the Bank of London of South America, on Rua da Alfândega, where he held a position for many years, since a bachelor could live reasonably on the salary at that time.

Sometimes I felt that he went unnoticed, and unfairly so. Whenever newspapers praised my brother Paulo [who became a renowned neurologist] or me, I felt like protesting that they had it all wrong: our brother Carlos Augusto was the best of us. At other times, seeing that Paulo and I, because of our successful careers, enjoyed amenities that Carlos lacked, it made me sad to think about his financial constraints.

How wrong I was! Although my brother led a rather modest life, he experienced neither the inevitable mood swings nor the alternating periods of leisure or crisis that constantly affected us. We worried about the superfluous, while he focused on the small things he hoped to obtain and that, once acquired, represented new highlights in his hermetic and orderly existence. He was an artisan, and as such he organized his life carefully, crafting it with the patience and love that we sometimes lacked, and thus lending it a more authentic and fair meaning.

He took great pleasure in buying his little house in Ipanema, which he never left, and in paying off the monthly installments. He derived such enthusiasm from gradually rebuilding it with his meager savings. Later there was the country house in Mendes that he slowly renovated. He himself planted the grass and trees, waiting happily for it all to grow like a long-cherished, almost impossible dream that was now coming true.

Occasionally I called him from Europe for no particular reason except the pleasure of our great friendship, to hear his voice and know that all was well with him. Upon my return to Brazil, despite being so nearby, we hardly ever saw each other. He was at home in Ipanema, and I was tied down by work to my Copacabana studio.

One morning my brother awoke feeling ill. Paulo called me and said in forewarning, "Come quickly. It's quite serious, there's nothing to be done."

Now I have only my sisters Lilia and Leonor, and my brother Paulo.

Paulo is my best friend. Sometimes I visit with him at his home in Barra–a splendid house surrounded by gardens, with a swimming pool and a soccer field. His children and grandchildren are always there, plunged in an enviable atmosphere of togetherness. I remember that years ago it was hard even to talk to him since he was always carrying a child in his arms, and there would be a couple of more kids hanging on to him. But the fruit of all that affection and caring is there to see in the beautiful friendships he nurtured.

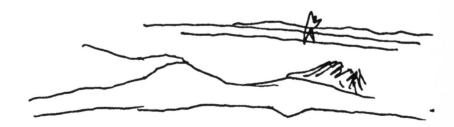

We sit by the pool and recall the old times when we had neighboring offices in the Porto Alegre building, and the pranks we played on each other, and his becoming a physician as almost a predestined mission in life. Everybody admired him; he was so polite and devoted to his patients, as his profession required. He felt deeply for the anguish of those who came from all over Brazil to seek his care. "It's not the surgeries that wear me out," he once told me, "but seeing the sick on the operating table, and being part of their suffering and their hopes."

It was then 1988. I felt unease at the ways of the world and at my life fading away, but it impressed me to see him so serene, accepting his fate as if life were just a fine, leisurely stroll, completed and made eternal only by the succession of new generations.

I spent five trouble-free years at the National School of Fine Arts and made some good friendships there: lifelong friends such as Hélio Uchôa, Milton Roberto, Carlos Bittencourt, João Cavalcanti, Fernando Saturnino de Brito,[22] and others. After the third year, like all my classmates I felt the need to get a job with a construction firm. This kind of work enabled the students to learn more about the profession—and the salary would also bring new opportunities.

Like most of my fellow students, I was reluctant to adapt to the commercial architecture that surrounded us. Despite financial difficulties, I preferred working without pay for Lúcio Costa and Carlos Leão,[23] who I hoped would assuage some of my doubts as an architecture student. Actually, they were doing me a favor. Furthermore, my choice showed that I was not hollow-headed and hasty: my goal was to become a good architect.

How I benefited from my early days with those dear friends! With them I learned to respect our colonial history, to appreciate beautiful old Portuguese buildings, so sober and rigid, with their thick walls of stone or *taipa de pilão* (gravel-clay wattle), their gently sloping slate tiles contrasting with their whitewashed walls. As far as architecture was concerned these buildings had nothing to offer but a good example. They were honest beyond reproach, as we all should be.

I remember Leão drawing beautiful women and talking about the world of the arts, laughing readily like the good companion he was; and Lúcio, a little more reserved, cautious and polite as always.

Of course, I was not really of much use to them. Even so, I already had the feeling that my calling was to be an architect. As I remember, it was during this period at Lúcio's office that I graduated as an architect and was first in the class together with Milton Roberto. I recall that when we had finished work on the first stage of the Mangueira university campus with Lúcio, he turned to Jorge Moreira[24] and said, "Jorge, you should not be earning more than Oscar. We shall have to combine the two amounts and share evenly." My immediate response was, "I would rather add up the three salaries, Jorge's, Reis's, and my own, and divide by three." My friend Reis was earning the same salary as I was. Lúcio concluded, "Oscar is a good fellow."

On several occasions Lúcio gave me support and encouragement that I never forgot and always sought to repay. When the chairman of the Brazilian Institute of Architecture, sent to me by Israel Pinheiro,[25] suggested in the presence of João Cavalcanti that they cancel the competition to choose a design for Brasília's master plan and instead bring in a team of urban planners, I did not hesitate to reply, "I will do all I can to keep that idea from going through." The proposal was discarded, and Lúcio Costa was chosen for the job.

It gives me particular satisfaction to recall Lucio's fine character: his unwavering professional verve, his appreciation of our colonial architecture, his enthusiasm for the work of Le Corbusier, his fine designs, the first-rate sketches that marked his talent as an architect, and his work on Brasília, which made him a discerning urban planner overnight.

I now have a portrait of Gustavo Capanema[26] in front of me, and, gazing at it, I am prompted to say something about this dear friend, about his cultivated learning and intelligence, his politeness–the scrupulous correctness cultivated by men in the public eye. The picture shows him looking at the Ministry of Education and Health building as it neared completion. He has a satisfied smile on his face, and with good reason, too. With this building and the opportune presence of Le Corbusier, Capanema gave Brazilian architecture the initial momentum it needed, dissolving misconceptions and demonstrating to everyone that modern techniques had imposed Modern architecture.

Capanema is gazing at the high, monumental *pilotis* that create free spaces, the *brise-soleil*, the functionally independent complex of exhibition spaces and auditorium between the columns. I sense that he was taking pleasure in all of this as he eyed the completion of the work that had brought him so many troubles. His was the satisfaction of a job well done, his the certainty that he had never lacked courage or determination, or unwavering optimism. Nevertheless, those were long and hard years, when he met with fierce opposition. Some said the building was "communist." Little did they know—such was the depth of their ignorance—that the Soviet Union had condemned Modernist architecture as a decadent expression of the capitalist bourgeoisie. Others accused him of betraying the customs and traditions of our own nation, as if life never moved on, as if Man and Nature were not constantly evolving.

My friend Capanema was able to withstand the pressure because he appreciated the importance of the work in the context of Brazilian architecture and the plastic arts. There were, of course, plenty of supporters too: Rodrigo, Lúcio, Drummond, Manuel Bandeira, Abgard Renault, Afonso Arinos, Prudente, Mário Andrade,[27] and so many others understood and encouraged him. Nevertheless, it was no easy task!

Capanema was a perfectionist; he not only attended to the global aspect of the work but also detailed the finishings, the colors of the walls, and the furniture. Even works of art were brought in at the right stage; this was a long-forgotten practice that he enthusiastically revived. To him we owe the magnificent murals by Cândido Portinari and the sculptures by Jacques Lipchitz, Celso Antônio, and Bruno Giorgi.[28] I remember him visiting Portinari's home in Laranjeiras and Celso Antônio's on-site atelier, and I recall his ecstatic admiration of their works in progress, his awe as he talked about them afterward.

His interests ranged far beyond the Ministry of Education and Health building. He also gave the best of himself to teaching, the plastic arts, and the preservation of our monuments. If it were not for Capanema, our historical and artistic legacy would have deteriorated and many historical building complexes in Ouro Preto, Congonhas, and Olinda would have been lost forever. He set up the National Historical and Artistic Heritage Service (SPHAN), ably managed by Rodrigo, which repaired existing works and put an end to the looting that had decimated Brazil's historic churches.

I was often summoned to Capanema's office and shared his friendship with Drummond, Leal Costa, João Massot, Carlos Cruz,[29] and so many others. From there we would go on to see the work— Celso Antônio's *O homem brasileiro* (Brazilian Man)—or lunch at the Cristal, or peruse minor renovations at his house in Santa Teresa.

Afterward, for several years we met in Brasília and recalled the old times and the pressures he had endured. We talked of the book he intended to write about his experience as minister of education, but his initial enthusiasm for writing soon waned due to his unrelenting perfectionism.

It gives me particular pleasure to recall how, unprompted, he interceded with the mayor of Brasília, a hidebound reactionary who had insisted on firing me from Novacap,[30] the organization charged with building the new capital. This was during the period of police repression under the Médici[31] military government, and I was away in Europe when I learned of his supportive gesture. He was no longer the minister of education and health I had met years before; now he was one of my best friends.

Not so long ago, in 1985, I wrote to the minister of education, Marco Maciel, to suggest that the ministry building be named after Gustavo Capanema. My friend Maciel replied, "This tribute does justice to the man who made it possible to build that magnificent work, that unique manifestation of creative freedom and the emblematic landmark of the new Brazilian architecture."

Jorge [Moreira], Reidy,[32] Hélio, and I moved out of our suite in Nilo Pecanha and set up offices in the Porto Alegre block, opposite the Ministry of Education. This was the most intense period of professional involvement we had ever experienced, but we were also wildly bohemian—which only goes to show, my friend, that there is no clash between these two lifestyles. We worked hard, but we always found time to have fun.

The office was always packed: there was Carlos Leão, Vinícius de Moraes, Echenique, Luiz Jardim, Eça, Galdino Duprat,[33] and Cavalcanti. . . There was also my brother Paulo, who had his medical office in the same building and shared a waiting room with our office. At the end of the day everybody got together as if it were a Saturday or Sunday. We "had a real good time," in the words of Damaso, a character in Eça de Queiroz's novel *A ilustre casa de Ramires* (The Illustrious House of Ramires).

Oh, what memories! We were all the best of friends and we certainly understood the importance of laughing at life, forgetting the precariousness of things, and imagining a better world to live in. We had no respect for prejudice and were not at all concerned with bourgeois society and its dogmas.

One night, Leão got drunk and made a huge erotic drawing on the office wall that remained there for several days, to the astonishment of visitors. We cared very little about what people might think of us— we were too young for that. Come evening, we would head for some bar to talk with friends, go over the day's problems and review works in progress, or chat with the women who appeared as the city's nightlife got underway.

I had a house built in the Mendes area for my father, but the place won me over, too. It was a quiet location in the Rio de Janeiro mountains, free from unexpected encounters and the impertinent beach-going socialite set. I picked a small lot on the road to Vassouras through which flowed a pleasant stream that, at that time, was swollen by seasonal rains. In just one month I built the house, making use of an old chicken coop that I split up into living room, bedrooms, kitchen, and so forth. The roofing was made of asbestos tiles and the facade was covered by a wooden trellis. The little house shaped up nicely as the creepers flowered, becoming almost an extension of the garden, homey and picturesque.

As I had intended, I spent carnival and other holidays there for several years. Through the low, horizontal living-room window, we could see the rapidly growing garden: the lawn, the clumps of bamboo trees, the bridge over the stream, the enormous *tecomas*–a gift from Nature that became our national tree– and the path winding up to the side road. But the house was somewhat lacking in terms of amusements, such as a swimming pool; fun at Mendes was limited to going "from the house to the bamboo trees and back," as our friend Eça commented jokingly. But the bamboos were pretty and I would lie there in a hammock, peering between the branches at the infinite spaces beyond, imagining myself in the desert like Saint-Exupéry, riding on the back of this old planet, roaming among the stars.

I liked Mendes for the privacy that Rio no longer offered. I liked to see my father happily riding his palomino-color horse there. He laughed and told his stories of a peaceful life that fate was to cut short–much too short, we thought. And I enjoyed seeing my family and grandchildren running around on the grass or driving the cart bravely dragged along by Mimoso the goat.

Occasionally we had company there; a friend was invited or somebody dropped by as they were going down the road. Abrecht or some other neighbor would come over for the unpretentious and undemanding small-town chatter that required little response and was limited to the minor troubles of those modest, resigned folk.

Sometimes we visited the home of my brother Carlos Augusto, our leader and counselor; or we would go to Aunt Alzira's whitewashed old colonial house, with its blue window frames and gently sloping roof in the Portuguese tradition, to bathe in the pool or walk around the lake or talk on the veranda, which was covered in enormous violet meadow saxifrage.

But the Rio state government decided to build a new highway alongside the old road. Earthmovers blocked the river, and over the years the small house at Mendes was flooded and was eventually destroyed. There was nothing we could do about it; this was during the dark years of Médici's rule.

Warm memories from our past were left behind in those damp-rotted walls.

I made several ocean voyages between Brazil, Europe, and the United States, since I did not like to fly. The voyage was a ten-day vacation on the wide ocean; no phone calls, no commitments whatsoever. I loved to gaze at the ocean, which changed from day to day; the vastness brought to my mind eternity. I liked those leisurely few days stretched out on a deck chair, reading or chatting, with no work to do.

One of these trips led me to Moscow, and on the way I took Annita and my friend Eça to see the Old World. We stopped off in Italy and saw Rome, Florence, Venice; then to Portugal to see Lisbon; then traveled to Paris, where Vinícius de Moraes met us at the station. We spent three days in Paris, a week in Czechoslovakia, a month in Berlin, and finally reached Moscow.

War could still be felt everywhere: half-destroyed cities, highways being rebuilt, the faces of individuals who could never forget the ordeal. But everywhere there was a need for hope, a desire for recovery. Czechoslovakia reminded me of the war and of old Kafka, whose books I had so appreciated, but our main destination was Moscow. We were eager to observe the October Revolution and its principles of justice and brotherhood that capitalism was determined to combat. And Moscow was not to disappoint us. What pleasure it gave us to walk around Red Square, impressed by the monumental Kremlin and the graceful vivacity of St. Basil's Cathedral with its golden domes!

We were happy to see that the people were getting over the war and building a society that would be fair and fraternal for all, according to the precepts of Marx and Lenin. We joined the long line

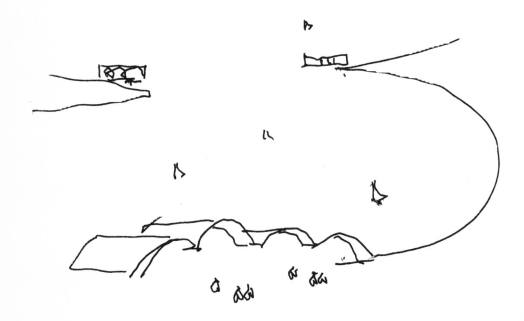

waiting to see the bodies of Lenin and Stalin, who were responsible for the victory of socialism and who now rested peacefully in their glass caskets.

A week later we left for Brazil with our memories of Paris, the Champs Elysées, the Left Bank, the ancient River Seine; Rome and its monuments; Venice, the piazza of San Marco packed as if it were a huge drawing room; Berlin, the Hotel Van Zoo, the Kaiser Wilhelm Church still standing; East Berlin, Stalin Avenue, the New Order emerging; and Moscow, the land of men who loved peace and liberty.

I was happy to see how Annita was enjoying the journey as she laughed at the pigeons covering her in the piazza of San Marco and felt warmly welcomed in the land of her forefathers. I was pleased to be able to give Eça–and [Galdino] Duprat, too–the opportunity to take a journey that they could only dream of. But whenever we asked old Eça what he thought of Moscow, he could not resist answering, "*Madureira sem bacanidade*" ("Like Madureira, but without its easygoing charm").[34]

My problem with air travel can cause significant distress: the disappointment of missing professional engagements–often important ones, too–and the inevitable inner frustration. Usually, when I commit to a trip I have every honest intention of fulfilling my promise. I pack my bag and leave early for the airport, but I tend to change my mind on the way there. After first seeing the trip as useful for the work involved, or as representing a kind and trusting invitation, I begin to reject it as an unnecessary and unbearable im-position. I become irritated with myself and anxiously wonder, "Why should I fly if it troubles me? Because it's important professionally?" And I begin to see the journey as a threat to my physical prerogatives and individual liberty, a despicable affair ruled by power and money.

So I don't go. I return home quite calmly. Later I tell my friends peremptorily, "I'll never fly again."

Later, however, chatting at the office, I will admit to the importance of the skipped journey, and I am overcome with a feeling of guilt and frustration. The next invitation sees me forgetting all about the problem and committing myself to plane travel once again, making a reservation and purchasing a ticket. Then the whole story is repeated. I can recall a few good examples of this contradictory state of mind.

On one occasion, Juscelino Kubitschek[35] was waiting to meet me at the airport and I had to send a laconic but firm message: "Mr. President, I'm not on the plane. Coming by road. Apologies." Fidel Castro, after a long and fruitless wait, joked with visiting friends, "Tell Niemeyer I'll send a ship to pick him up from Brazil." My old friend Agildo Barata,[36] ever an optimist, once told his PCB comrades, "I've talked with Oscar. This time he is going to the conference in Europe." Assis Chateaubriand,[37] whom I once left waiting for me in Recife, later smiled and told me: "You behaved like a good Communist." And the same story repeated itself over the years. The only time I will unhesitatingly get on a plane is when I am in Europe and need to get back to Brazil, but there is no ship sailing.

Another time, I received a commission to design the Administrative Center for Pernambuco in Recife from my considerate, cordial friend Marco Marciel, and I accepted his invitation to visit the site. I did not want to fly there. There was a northbound Italian ship that called at Salvador, so I planned to land there and spend a few days with Lelé[38] seeing the beautiful buildings he was executing in the city. Then Maciel would send a car for me, and I would take the coastal road, stopping for an occasional dip in the ocean and a sip of coconut water. Eventually I would show up in the capital of Pernambuco.

Everything went off quite well. The ocean voyage was pleasant and relaxing. Lelé showed me his architecture and then I headed for the beaches of the Northeast with their coconut palms swinging in the breeze and the ocean beckoning us every day.

Once I was in Paris at the home of my friend Dimanche, and a samba by Ataulfo Alves, "A professorinha" (The Little School Teacher), was playing on the phonograph. There was nothing special about it, nothing that should have made me feel so emotional. It was just a good samba, in which Ataulfo affectionately sang of his old teacher. I do not know why, but that song was so typically Brazilian that it made me think of home and friends and my distant family. To my embarrassment, I felt a great need to cry, and tears welled up inside my chest. On some pretext I went out to the balcony and allowed myself to weep to my heart's content.

I experienced this feeling on several occasions when I was abroad. An enormous sadness came over me, and I was struck by remorse, feeling the despair of being so far away from everybody,

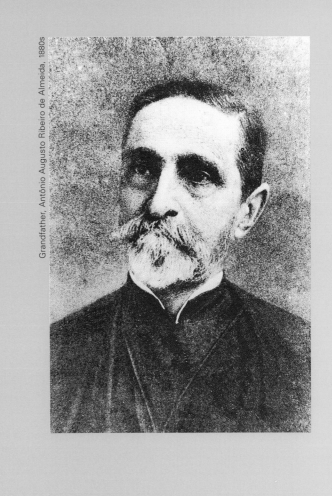

Grandfather, Antônio Augusto Ribeiro de Almeida, 1880s

Father, Oscar Niemeyer Soares, and mother, Delphina Ribeiro de Almeida Niemeyer Soares, 1890s

Mother, Delphina Ribeiro de Almeida Niemeyer Soares, 1890s

Grandmother, Maria Eugénia Ribeiro de Almeida, 1890s

Cousin Milota, née Emilia Adelaide de Veiga de Almeida Albuquerque, 1880s

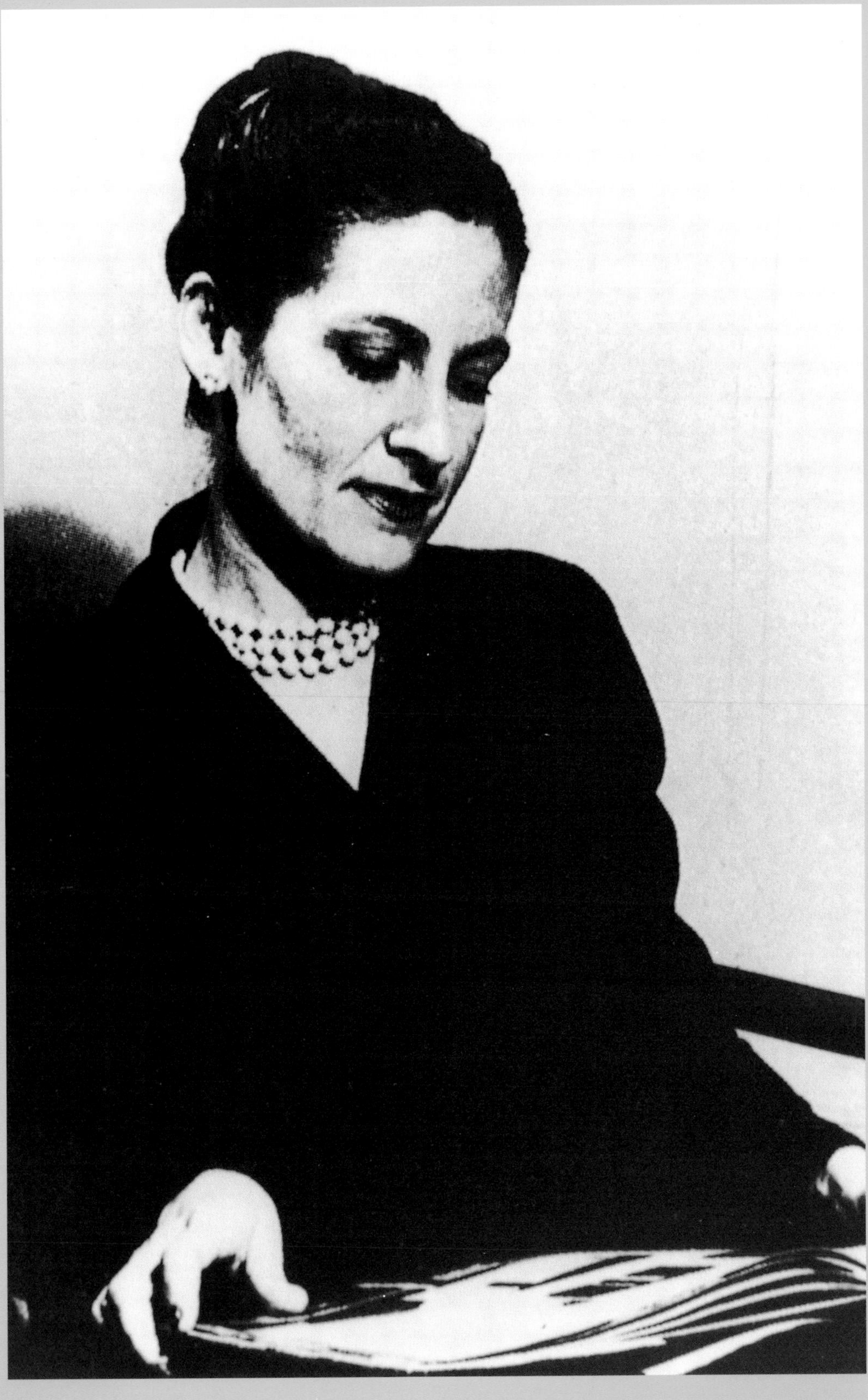

Wife, Annita Niemeyer, ca.1950

Niemeyer's family. Standing, from left: brother Carlos Augusto, mother, and father. Seated, from left: sisters Lilia and Leonor, Oscar Niemeyer, sister Judith, and brother Paulo, 1920s

Niemeyer with his wife, Annita, Paris, 1954

certain that they too were affected. Sometimes this also occurred at happy moments, when I was relaxed and enjoying good conversation. A remark, any random word, could set me off. But usually it happened when I thought of my friends, and with a heavy heart I became homesick and filled with regret. I felt the urge to drop everything and go back to Brazil.

So there you have my dominant motivations, family, friendships, the beaches, and the hills of my country.

For many years I nurtured a sound friendship with Rodrigo M. F. de Andrade, a cultivated man who was generous in his life and his relationships. I was a regular guest at his home in Copacabana. Together, we often visited the historic towns of Minas Gerais. We shared the same friendships and joys. What an extraordinary friend! I used to call on him practically every week. There I would meet Prudente de Morais Neto, Manuel Bandeira, Gastão Cruls, Nava,[39] Reis, and his wife, Graciema, who always welcomed us kindly. During carnival we even met at his home for the traditional parties with pranks and games. But he was also very busy with his work for the National Historical and Artistic Heritage Service (SPHAN), a cause to which he was passionately devoted throughout his life.

I recall our first journey to Ouro Preto, and Rodrigo inspecting the the new hotel site beside Saint Francis Church. Ouro Preto is remarkable, and not only for its churches. Its most important feature is the historical ambience it has preserved, which takes curious visitors back to the heroic gold-rush era of Vila Rica. The town is known for its steep streets carved into the hill slopes, paved with cobblestones, and lined with whitewashed row houses, their nearly identical windows stone-framed or blue-painted; it is also known for the characteristic rake of its sloping roofs, and for the churches on the most prominent sites, fine baroque buildings like their Portuguese counterparts. The town is frozen in time. Its people wend their way up and down its hills and still have time to sit in a café and chat. This was in the heyday of Toffolo's hotel and restaurant, of his son-in-law, Epaminondas, and of a fellow there–I forget his name–who ran home everyday at six o'clock to set off fireworks in fulfillment of some weird vow.

I had always conceived of Ouro Preto as being free from automobiles, which would be left in parking lots on the outskirts of the town. I realized that this would present problems and that getting around would be uncomfortable for some people; but, on the other hand, everyone would get a better feeling for the town. I recall Rodrigo talking about these matters and about Aleijadinho,[40] the houses that might tumble, and the urbanization programs that threatened their preservation as official landmarks. This was my friend's lifelong concern; he devoted his life to historic preservation issues, which affected not only Ouro Preto but Brazil as a whole.

This old, dear friend of mine was so valuable to me! I often went to his place early in the morning and we would ride into town together. We chatted about everything, and time and again about the hubbub we created at the office. Rodrigo was as curious as Prudente; he always asked for detailed accounts, but no sooner would I start telling him than I would have to pause momentarily.

On our way downtown we stopped to visit his mother, whom he went to see every morning. Back in the car after asking for her blessing, Rodrigo would return to the point in the conversation where we had left off. Whenever I told him about a negative experience or someone lining up against me, he would interject in solidarity: "That son of a bitch!" As he saw it, his friends were always in the right. He was the epitome of a friend, as Manuel Bandeira used to say.

In 1986, the Ministry of Education and Culture awarded the Rodrigo M. F. de Andrade Medal to a number of individuals, including

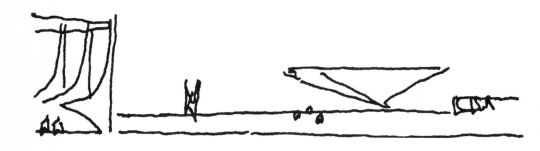

me. Deeply moved, I told Graciema, "This is the medal that I have been happiest to receive." This was true. I keep the other medals in a drawer, but this one I always have at hand.

As time went by, I began to feel rather ill-informed about non-architectural issues (like most of my colleagues), so I decided to improve my knowledge of the world. I recall Rodrigo's words of advice: "Read the Greeks and the Portuguese classics, Oscar." So I did. I read a great deal of them, thirsting for knowledge and wanting to know everything. I read them as eagerly as I had read the work of Le Corbusier years before.

Following my friend's advice, I began with the Greeks. I was curious about the discourses of Socrates and Plato; I was amazed at the intelligent manner in which they built their astute dialogues of exemplary consistency. Next, I tackled the Portuguese classics–Diogo do Couto, Fernão Lopes,[41] and others who described the pillages along the African coast and the shootouts that put an end to them. The authors used the simple, concise, and direct language that Rodrigo so much appreciated. Out of my keen interest in literature, I slowly and carefully read Vieira's speeches and the writings of Herculano, Eça de Queiroz, and Machado de Assis.[42] Herculano employed a severe language; Queiroz was at times baroque, though full of wit and spontaneity. Oh, how I still refer to *Os Maias* (The Maya) or *A ilustre casa de Ramires* (The Illustrious House of Ramires), and Machado de Assis, whose irony permeated the souls of his characters!

I had no literary claims. All I wanted was to be able to explain my designs in writing in a simple and straightforward manner. And so I read on, bent over the literature of Brazil and Portugal, pondering each author's weight and talent. I read from Machado de Assis to the more recent writers of these two countries. I was enthusiastic about the simplicity of some, the imagination and spontaneity of others, and the sociopolitical awareness of those permanently concerned with individuals stricken by poverty. Finally, when I turned to foreign authors, I was surprised by the literary consistency of Camus; the intelligence and erudition of André Malraux; the investigation of the human being by Freud, Kafka, and Dostoyevsky; the guilelessness of Gide and Chekhov; the realism of Henry Miller; the alertness and talent of Proust; and the magnificence of Russian writers such as Tolstoy, Chekhov, Dostoyevsky, and Gorky.

Intuitively, however, I always felt that literature was not enough for me; I needed to become more familiar with the world in which we live, and I had to learn the reason for our existence on this ancient planet of ours. I became attracted to such subjects as life, genetics, and the cosmos. I learned considerably from the writings of Max Jacob and Jacques Monod,[43] as well as from Sartre, who tries to convince us that life is a big flop while explaining his existentialism as being "the prevalence of the being's existence over essence."

In my spare time I read textbooks by Celso Cunha,[44] and the great masters of poetry, including Baudelaire with his love poems and Neruda with his revolutionary call.

I did not allow myself to criticize or assume radical positions. I read out of curiosity. I read with equal respect the novels by Gabriel Garcia Márquez, Jorge Amado, or Anatole France, and poems by Apollinaire, Carlos Drummond de Andrade, and Ferreira Gullar.[45] From each of them I took a different type of enjoyment, as if I were standing before a painting by Matisse or Picasso. I was even attracted to Simenon's detective novels, much to the chagrin of our so-called intellectuals–whom I once left dumbfounded by quoting from Sartre's *Lettres au Castor*, in which he announced with pleasure, "Today I read three books by Simenon."

Every time I became attracted to an author I tried to read his or her personal mail. I learned a good many things reading the letters exchanged between Lenin and Gorky and Chekhov, or the memoirs of André Gide, Luís Buñuel, and many others. Personally, I prefer simple, everyday language. "Literature is enhanced when it comes close to oral language," Alberto Moravia[46] once stated during an interview. If on the one hand I was thrilled with books on social issues, on the other hand books with an entirely different content also attracted me. I was lured by the multiple attributes of literary purity, though I agree that the combination of both could be even more enriching. But beauty has always prevailed! I remember this magnificent stanza by Ricardo Jaimes Freyre,[47] transcribed in a book by Jorge Luís Borges:

Peregrina Paloma imaginaria
Que enardeces los últimos amores,
Alma hecha de luz, de música y de flores,
Peregrina Paloma imaginaria.

"Imaginary Peregrine Dove
That rekindles lost loves
Soul made of light, music and flowers,
Imaginary Peregrine Dove."

Borges remarked of these words, "These verses mean absolutely nothing. But to me they are unforgettable."

In 1944 we moved our office again, this time from Passeio Público to a house that I inherited from my cousin Milota on Rua Conde Lages. A former Rio de Janeiro mayor and relative, Pereira Passos, had suggested she purchase the property. He himself had bought the house next door, which still belongs to his grandsons, Antônio Fernando and Felisberto Bulhões Carvalho. Although we did not stay there long, it was much better working in a house than in the downtown building where our previous offices had been.

In this spacious house with french windows opening onto the street, with enhanced privacy and quiet surroundings, we felt as if we were in one of the older Rio districts. From the windows, we could watch passersby and hear the familiar vendors' cries: "Grinder, Grinder. . .," "Buy my Soberano caramel candies," "Ice cream man, ice cream man. . .," "Sell me your secondhand men's clothing. . . ." These were the traditional colorful characters who featured in all chronicles of city life. Botafogo had also been home to bohemian residents in the past; consequently, we often spotted hookers and homosexuals in the streets, old-timers who still lived in the neighborhood.

The house included living and dining rooms and ten bedrooms—some of which had been added at a later date, when the number of bedrooms became very important to the function and purpose of the house. I very much liked the house and remembered how, many years before, while still a pupil at the Barnabite School, I often roamed the neighboring streets with classmates. I recall the bar on the corner, the man playing the mandolin, the women walking along the streets, putting on airs of insubordination. Mainly, I remember how we had been attracted to that strange area, which we schoolboys saw brimming with mystery, brawls, and libertine characters.

I had never been a member of the Communist Party, although I had made donations to Red Aid. I remember the day, possibly in 1935, when Honório de Freitas Guimarães, a long-standing member of the party, came to my home in Ipanema to collect a bundle of clothes. How I admired him, a wealthy man who had given up everything for the revolution!

It was while I worked at the house on Rua Conde Lages that I came into contact with Luís Carlos Prestes and his comrades, and on listening to their stories of struggle and sacrifice, one day I made a decision: "Prestes, you keep the house. Your task is far more important than mine." So the old house on Rua Conde Lages, first a family home, then a police station, later a brothel, and then an architecture office, became the Metropolitan Committee of the PCB, of which I became a permanent member.

It was the 1950s and you could hardly imagine a more varied group of friends than ours. There were so many different and controversial characters that only the common denominator of great friendship could hold us together.

I miss Walter Garcia Lopes (the one we called Eça), a native of Franca in the rural interior of the state of São Paulo, who turned up one day in the company of Fernando Brito. He was an avid reader and his pockets were bursting with newspapers and magazines. He was full of resentment toward bourgeois prejudice and fought it with the style and language of a man from the rural interior. He treated everybody in exactly the same manner, whether they were important people or his pals from the newsstand. He was poor, but his was a dignified poverty that despised the false self-importance of the wealthy. He had sold his land in Entre Rios and spent the proceeds in the clubs of Rio, where he made many friends, or on his lovers in the Lapa district. His Chaplinesque romances and attempts to reform his lovers often resulted in quarrels and brawls.

For some time, Eça was short of money and lived at our office. It was then that I got him a job in the Department of Mineral Production. After a few days there, his boss, a Roman Catholic and a bureaucrat, hearing Eça happily recounting his exploits, could not resist protesting: "Senhor Walter, when you go home at the end of the day, do you not think of Brazil?" "All I think about is screwing around," came the reply meant to annoy him. But this was far from the truth. In fact, our friend was very much concerned with the country's future, and one of his favorite pastimes was to hold heated political debates. We stuck together and even traveled around Brazil together.

Prudente de Morais Neto, whom we called Prudentinho, was befriended by one and all. If any of us saw him on the street, we would take him off to a café, eager to hear his stories. Eça would fake naïvete and tell tall tales. "The first time I got laid," he would say, "was quite amusing. I was tucked well inside the woman and ready to drop off to sleep when she cried out, 'Hey! What do you take me for? A drawer?!'" He would boast of his adventures in Lapa and recount stories of a boxer friend of his and the fights he got into. He did actually get into a brawl on one occasion, and I was shocked to see his face covered in bandages.

How delightful it was to share his company! Some time later, in Brasília, where I had managed to get him and his wife into one of the low-income housing projects, he began to feel ill and sent for Sabino: "If I get this pain again, I won't make it," he said. The pain returned and took our friend away forever.

I have already mentioned our trips around the country, and I am now going to tell you about one of them. This was the longest of them all, to the state of Rio Grande do Sul.

It was in October 1944 and Fernando Brito, Gauss Estelita, and I were in front of our office on Rua Conde Lages, getting our car—a 1930 Ford that was falling to pieces—ready for the seven-hundred-

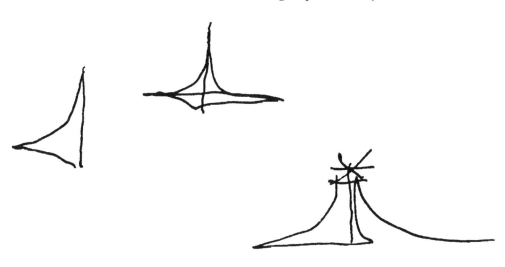

mile drive to Porto Alegre. As they waved from the window our colleagues burst into laughter–understandably, since this was a very long way to go for an old jalopy. Of course, it would have been better to go by plane, but that would have lent our trip a businesslike, energetic, and organized tone that was not to our liking. We were happy to travel this way, not knowing when we would arrive or, indeed, if we would arrive at all. So we breezily set out on our journey.

A few hundred yards down the road, on the corner of Conde Lages and Gloria, the car suddenly stalled and Fernando, who was driving, got out to check the engine. He opened the hood and stroked his mustache. He checked the gasogene,[48] fiddled with the carburetor, and yanked at a few wires and cables. Since he knew nothing about mechanics, however, he carefully announced, "We had better leave tomorrow." So we went back to the office, unloaded all the gear, and laughed as we planned to set out again the following day.

As a precaution we decided to go first to Botafogo to see Contra-Pino the mechanic, who got the car going, gunned the engine a few times, and declared, "Ready to roll." Feeling worried after the events of the previous day, I ventured the question, "Do you think we can make it to Porto Alegre?" "Might make it as far as São Paulo!" he replied. We looked at each other, got into the car, and took off.

It was a beautiful day and the car sped along the Rio de Janeiro–São Paulo highway. We were like the Three Musketeers, everything looking just fine and dandy, when suddenly the sky clouded over and a storm broke out. What rotten luck! Rain poured down, hailstones clattered on the ground, and lightning flashed across the horizon ahead of us as the day suddenly darkened. Our windshield wipers froze, the windows steamed up, and the engine power dwindled. We were nervously attempting to avoid careening off the highway when we came to the forty-eight kilometer mark and saw the School of Agronomy campus (now the Rural University), so we decided to stop and talk to the principal, who would surely understand our plight. He did.

We woke up very early the next day. The sky was clear, the morning crisp and pleasant, and our old Ford was rested and once again speeding gallantly along the highway. "We'll be in São Paulo by evening," said Fernando. However, the gasogene failed several times and it was night before we reached Jacareí, still a ways from São Paulo. Estelita burst out, "Fuck! Twelve hours to go to Jacareí and Fernando told us we would be in São Paulo by evening! What can we do all night in Jacareí? The light in the hotel is too dim to read by and there are no girls here. Oh, shit." To which Fernando smiled and replied, "Take it easy Estelita. It's not far to São Paulo, we'll be there tomorrow." In fact, we did make it to São Paulo the next night, and we booked into the Savoya Hotel. It had taken us two days to get that far.

We were all in a fine mood the following morning, and after a shower and breakfast we set out to hire a cab, since the old Ford was on its last legs. In Praça Republica, we chose the taxi that seemed to be in the best shape. "Would you drive us to Rio Grande do Sul?" we asked the driver. "At your service!" replied Pale Pale, who now has a boarding house in São Paulo called Pensão do Pale Pale.

We went back to the hotel and found Rodrigo M. F. de Andrade looking for us. When we went up to our room Rodrigo laughed in surprise, realizing we were all three staying in the same room. "You look like a bunch of kids on vacation!" he said. And he was right, but we liked being together and talking long into the night, discussing the day's events and our plans for the following day.

We were always like that, even much later, when we rented an apartment in São Paulo, on the same Praça de Republica, and slept on canvas cots scattered around the rooms. And what a great time we had then! Sometimes there were six or eight of us together there and the place was like a hostel. Friends dropped by, girls hung around, and our apartment became a festive party. Silioma,[49] our dear colleague Silioma, lived there permanently and as often as not we would arrive from Rio to find him in the company of his favorite mulatto girls. I remember how one of them was chatting to me one day and told me confidentially, "Of all the boys that come here, I prefer Dr. Silioma. He kisses us on the lips."

Rodrigo took us to lunch and talked about the National Historical and Artistic Heritage Service and the huge problems it faced, and said he wanted to return to Rio. What a great friend he was! He was concerned about our arrangements for the journey; was the cab a good one, were the highways blocked. "You had best take the mountain route, the seaboard route is crap!" he advised.

The following morning, as agreed, we waited for Pale Pale at the hotel. The clock struck ten and there was no sign of him. Fernando and Estelita complained, "Jerk! You paid him in advance and we got stiffed. Pale Pale won't turn up." Soon after that, however, to our great surprise, he did turn up, accompanied by a tall, shy young man. "Sorry. We ate pork-and-bean stew last night, got drunk out of our minds, and woke up late. This is Miguel, my assistant."

We thought this was all very amusing. These people were so easygoing! We put the baggage in the comfortable, but rather worn

1936 Chevrolet and drove off. Pale Pale was in a cheerful mood and soon broke into Italian song while his assistant, Miguel, glowered at us and was about as talkative as a fish. An hour later, the car came to a halt–the gasogene had failed. We got out to change the charcoal, and after much effort, we were soon underway again. We felt a little pessimistic but Pale Pale seemed so self-assured and confident that we set off once again without a care in the world.

At noon, we stopped for lunch in Capão Bonito at a one-story boarding house that was none too clean. We drank some wine and ate chicken and rice. The town consisted of low-lying houses and dusty streets. When we got back into the car it refused to budge. Shit! It was the gasogene again. Pale Pale calmly opened the hood but then cut his finger as he fiddled with the cooling fan. He was bleeding profusely, so we stayed in the car while he went to the corner pharmacy to attend to it. Soon he was laughing again, despite the bandaged finger, and he got back to repairing the fan.

Suddenly we heard him yell "You son-of-a-bitch!" and we stared, in shock, as he leapt around in front of us with his finger in flames. The bandages had caught fire and we could only laugh as he picked up the screwdriver and screamed, "I'll smash this damn thing to pieces!" We got out of the car and, after some effort, succeeded in calming him down.

We continued on our journey. Pale Pale forgot the fan and sang loudly. The trip felt good again and we were having fun, happily listening to Pale Pale singing, when suddenly the car stopped once more. We all cursed the gasogene. What a piece of crap! However, Pale Pale explained that it had been the dampness, and it wouldn't break down again. This "dampness" explanation reassured us and the journey continued cheerfully, as if nothing out of the ordinary had happened. By afternoon we arrived at a small hotel in Apicaí, a horrible place where we once again ate chicken and rice. "Hell!" said Fernando, "They sure eat enough chicken around here!" We went to look at the rooms. There were three beds with grimy sheets, and the floor was all stained. Suspecting cockroaches, I suggested keeping the light on. But there were no cockroaches. I was just settling down in bed when I spotted dozens of bedbugs scurrying over the mattress like an army of madmen. I woke Estelita, who was groggy from sleep, and told him there were bugs in my bed. He grabbed a pillow and said, "Sleep in my bed, I'll sleep with them." Of course there were bugs in his bed, too, so I sat down in a corner until I fell asleep.

We left early the next morning but the car broke down again before we reached Curitiba. Pale Pale looked discouraged and we tried to cheer him up. Disguising our impatience, we went over and sat on the grass, exhausted, and stayed there laughing and telling stories until the gasogene was repaired. The area's rich natural landscape surrounded us; there were carefully tended fields and fences, mostly cattle pastures. We continued on our way and the surroundings began to take on a European appearance. Now the houses looked different; they became clean and civilized, with their high-peaked roofs. There were swastikas everywhere and signs in German, which angered us. This was the pro-German influence that was spreading around the state of Santa Catarina, until Getúlio[50] implemented his timely nationalist measures.

We reached Joinville, and the following day, after the gasogene had broken down three more times, we got to Blumenau. The next stretch of highway crossed arable land and tilled fields that alternated with old pine groves. Along the highway we saw picturesque estates, and there were grapes for sale in one of the driveways, so we bought a basket. The grapes were "divine," as Jacinth says of a plate of peas in Eça de Queiroz's novel *A Cidade e as Serras* (The City and the Mountains). And so it was, eating our grapes, that we reached Vacaria, to be greeted by a man wearing the region's traditional *bombachas* [flared calf-length riding pants], looking as if he had been expecting us. "Don't you people know the traffic rules?" he barked. "You must be from Curitiba!" The car was parked in a deserted square, in front of a barbecue restaurant lined with a uniform row of low-lying houses. We got out and explained to the man (who turned out to be the local police chief) that we were from Rio, and that we had not realized that there was one-way traffic in such a deserted square. He was understanding and, smiling, invited us to come for lunch at his nearby ranch, which we did–after a few beers with him and a group of locals who kindly kept us company. The barbecue was good and so was the hospitality, in the fine tradition of the noble gauchos. We all got drunk and had a great time in his company. It was already evening when we finally parted after an exchange of embraces and a round of lively cries of "Viva!" We drove off toward the south.

No sooner had we reached Serra das Antas [mountain range] than a storm erupted. What a downpour! A whole river of mud flowed down the slope and around the car. "Why didn't we take the seaboard route?" said Estelita. "You all fell for Rodrigo's ruse and now we are really screwed." And what a godforsaken road that was! We battled on up the mountain under the rain and lightning. On the right was the cliff edge. An enormous chasm opened up before our horrified eyes. The car was sliding along on mud and skidding all over the road. A terrified Miguel jumped onto the running board and, almost in tears, cried out, "I don't want to die, I have kids at home to look after!" I was scared, too, and suggested to Estelita that we jump out. But that would have been even worse. What were we going to do in the middle of the storm on that deserted mountainside? Pale Pale was terrified and kept the gas pedal to the floor, saying over and over, "Can't stop! Can't stop!" We made it down to the deserted plateau area and there was still no horizon to be seen. The rain kept pouring down in buckets, the wind whipped the trees along the roadside and howled and screeched through the windows. We pulled up our jacket collars and slept until morning, when we woke with the sun shining directly on our faces. The storm was over and we drove on to Porto Alegre in the gentle shade of the trees lining the highway, forgetting about the ordeals of the journey, back to thinking what a wonderful trip it was.

A nice hotel room had been booked, so we decided to stay there, all five of us, and we got our luggage out of the trunk. It had taken us nine days to get from Rio de Janeiro to Porto Alegre.

What of it? If we had traveled by plane there would have been no story to tell. We would not have seen the southern region of Brazil, we would have missed out on the fine countryside and the conviviality of our hospitable southern compatriots, we would not have met Pale Pale or Miguel, and we certainly would not have laughed so much.

"Hello, Dr. Niemeyer? Dr. Azambuja's aide is waiting for you downstairs." He was a pleasant and understanding young man. "Dr. Niemeyer, I have come to show you around our city. We may begin by visiting the electric power plant."

What a bore! We favored doing things ourselves, without guides or pre-established itineraries. There we were, exhausted after nine days on the road, and they wanted us to see the power station! It was really too much. "Listen pal," I said, "why don't we do something that's a little more fun? Where do the girls hang out in this town?" "Well," replied the young man, "yes, of course. But I am a little removed from that kind of thing myself." We persisted, "So what about Eloá's joint?" That did the trick. "Good idea!" he answered, and we guessed that he was her regular customer.

We spent the whole afternoon at Eloá's. After that, we often had lunch or dinner there, and whenever we had to go off and see Azambuja we could hardly wait to get back. Eloá's place had a garden and latticework out front. The house was pleasant and Eloá was charming. Without ceremony we went in and sat down. The girls came into the room and there was an inevitable moment of

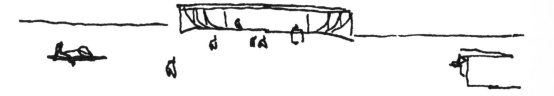

embarrassment. One girl was less inhibited and crossed her legs to show off everything she had below her belly button. Then she got up and put a record on the phonograph, an Argentine tango. And up jumped our guide all fired up for a dance. Damn, what a hypocrite!

The girls were all shapely and pretty; they had the baroque buttocks that we favored, and a natural and homespun air. Though we had a look at the downtown area and the main streets of Porto Alegre, our main effort in getting to know the region and interacting with its native people had been redirected to Eloá's place.

The return trip was not much different, though mostly by the seaboard route. There were no major problems and our guide had very little work to do. Once again the gasogene broke down regularly and Pale Pale had his tantrums, and once again we happily got on with the journey after the incidents, as if nothing had happened.

Eight days later we were back in São Paulo. I was beginning to get used to São Paulo and not long after that, Otavio Frias[1] asked me to do some architectural work there. It is always a pleasure to recall our friendship. I remember him inviting us to lunch at his home, and then excusing himself to take his customary siesta after the meal. We remained in the room talking and half-an-hour later he reappeared, refreshed and ready to get on with his schedule, which frequently went on past midnight.

Oh, those nostalgic memories of our office in Rio, of our hellraising and carousing, and the journeys from Rio to São Paulo or Brasília. . . how I would like to be able tell you all about them!

Of course we enjoyed ourselves: there were girls coming around, and we had all the fun that young people deserve. We endured criticism on account of the usual prejudices, yet we got on with our work at the same time, and we had our ambitions, and we took on our responsibilities.

So while I cannot write all I would like to about those times, it is pleasant to recall them a little, remembering old companions and that almost juvenile optimism that came to us so naturally. Oh, yes, they sure were the good old days! Carlos Leão, Eça, Galdino Duprat, Carlos Echenique, Fernando Brito, Reis, Jorge Moreira, Reidy. . . all so far away now. Such good friends and such solidarity. Everyone ready to pitch in if any one of us was faced with momentary adversity!

And what of Cinira? She was there having fun with us too, her beautiful body shaped in the baroque style we favored. How sad it is to feel that all that is fading away, as distant as life itself! Such an old and beloved friend, so generous and cheerful; I can almost hear her vivacious, carefree laughter now.

Of course, work often kept us busy, too, and we often stayed at our drawing board night after night, until the early hours of the morning. But then we would be so happy to lock up the office and go and have some fun together.

One day, a guy we didn't know too well came to the office, and there he was, really and truly getting on our nerves with his incredible nonchalance. Fernando decided to cut out four cardboard phalluses, and slowly and carefully he stuck them on the heels of the visitor's shoes. This strange character finished his business with us and we laughed as he proceeded along Avenida Rio Branco, unable to figure out why everyone was staring at him and laughing at the unusual spurs he was wearing.

I recall, too, on another occasion, Fernando sitting there, slowly squashing bananas and dropping them out of the office window on passersby. Down below, there was a crowd of people looking up at our friend, who remained unruffled, as if he had nothing to do with the whole business. Occasionally, he would fire my handgun into the ocean and wave it at Gauss Estelita, who would scream in terror, "Son of a bitch! One day you'll aim at the ocean and hit me." This was the bohemian side of life that the adversity of time has left behind.

I recall a time I was at the Aeronautics Center in the town of São José dos Campos, and José Lopes,[52] who did not know how to drive, wanted to try his hand with my pickup truck. As there was a wooden pile supporting the shed behind the car, I decided to play a practical joke on him. "Have a go at it then," I said as he got behind the steering wheel, and I added, "Put her in reverse!" He demolished the shed.

One night, we were sitting at a table with several Air Force officers and we decided to scare Duprat, who believed in ghosts. We set up the table for a séance and Estelita attached some string to a glass. When it began to move, Duprat, who had refused to take part in the session, got up and cried out, "It's just a game for you guys, but that glass is moving. This is a really important phenomenon!" Everyone burst out laughing and our companion, realizing that a trick had been played on him, angrily walked out and slammed the door shut and shouted that we were a bunch of real bastards. Later that night, in the dorm, there was a game on and Duprat stood in front of my bed shouting, "You bastards want to have some fun? Go to the movies!"

It's all gone now! Just memories of the passing years, youth gone forever.

But life goes on and here we are, esteemed readers, pretending to believe in things of no real consequence, dressed in the guise of an architect, and with a devotion to architecture that is wholly out of place in this unjust world.

Even today I have fond memories of my contacts with the PCB and the tasks assigned to me by the party: selling *Tribuna Popular*, the party newspaper; putting up posters and banners around the city; organizing cell meetings in the Gávea district, and later at the Central Committee headquarters in the Gloria neighborhood. I remember the meetings and rallies I helped organize and the pressures on all of us involved there as we faced numerous threats. Our tasks were sometimes difficult, but official orders were unquestioned and it would have been unthinkable not to carry them out.

The cell leaders, however, were not always competent and were often distinguished by an unrealistic authoritarianism. I recall the night Getúlio was overthrown and we received orders to hold cell meetings and offer whatever support possible. We were to organize resistance. All night long I ferried comrades around the city. On the last trip, at four o'clock in the morning, I took a member of my cell, a tall mulatto who carried a revolver wrapped in newspaper, to the downtown area and dropped him off in the Gloria district. I gave him some money and went back to my cell. The only comment from the cell's organizing secretary was, "I thought that you had done the same as Cavalcanti and just went home." I did not like that remark at all. Perhaps I should have done that, too.

One day, just before the party became legal, I came across Diógenes Arruda,[55] who waved at me on Avenida Beira-Mar. "Take these banners and help prepare for the rally!" he said. I joined in with my usual readiness to help. The meeting was supposed to be held in the Castelo quarter, but in fact that was impossible, as police cars were swarming around and confiscating the banners we had just placed there.

Many of my party comrades became lifelong friends, among them my dear friend Agildo Barata who was a Communist at heart. Now and then he liked to spend time talking to friends and enjoying himself while momentarily forgetting his revolutionary mission in life. Hunted by the political police, he always found a way to meet me for a talk or a poolside lunch at the Copacabana Palace hotel. His hat was his only disguise, but he shrugged off the danger and laughed with me as we talked of all kinds of subjects. He realized that nobody would think of looking for him at such a bourgeois place.

For Barata, every provocation deserved a response, as you may judge from these two episodes in his life. In 1935, along with several other people, he was arrested and taken to the army barracks. One of the more aggressive officers screamed at them, "Where's this son of a bitch Agildo Barata?" He stepped forward and introduced himself; "I'm Agildo Barata. You're the son of a bitch."

Many years afterward, João Saldanha tells me, the political police decided to break up a meeting in the Castelo quarter and arrest Agildo, who was organizing the event. Prestes began to speak and Agildo stuck a pistol in a policeman's gut and said, "Wait till Prestes finishes the speech, or I'll shoot you." Episodes such as these–and there are many more that affected our comrades–encouraged us as we went about our duties for the PCB.

I cannot think of Belo Horizonte without mentioning Carlos Echenique–a true friend, always there for me. I recall how funny he was, how he knew how to invent his romances, since women were a

constant concern of his, even when one day he had his leg in a plaster cast and asked me to lend him my apartment. I recall how he came with us on journeys, even though he was not part of our office staff. He liked our company and we loved him in spite of a few minor faults that we carefully tried to avoid.

Oh, old Echenique... How I miss you! One day, back in the 1940s, Governor Benedito Valadares[54] summoned me to Belo Horizonte. On the night before the meeting, Echenique took me to a nightclub in the city. It was a modest but entertaining nightclub, with a huge lounge divided by a long wooden trellis. We drank a great deal and at one point, with Echenique on one side of the trellis and me on the other, I decided to scare him by toppling the trellis. It collapsed with a roar, filling the whole nightclub with dust. The police came and, as my friend had a red handkerchief around his neck (the traditional symbol of a regional rebellion that had taken place there), he protested, claiming he was a gaucho. The local police in the state of Minas Gerais nurtured an intense dislike of gauchos, however, and within five minutes we were thrown out of the club and into the street.

So we spent our first night in Belo Horizonte at the jailhouse, trying to explain to the local chief of police what had happened.

Even in Brasília, Echenique followed me around on the pretext of selling marble traded by his friend Nápole.[55] One day, he called me urgently from Rio. He wanted to see me. He was feeling very ill. Overcome by emotion, we embraced each other for the last time.

Belo Horizonte! What an unusual city it was! It still had a tradition of hospitality, and lush vegetation shaded the main avenue; there were none of the traffic problems that it has today.

I loved staying at the Grande Hotel and eating in its glass-domed restaurant or drinking a draft beer in the corner bar while I waited for friends to show up. I often spent time there talking to Rodrigo [M. F. de Andrade] and Milton Campos,[56] or Teixeirão and my office colleagues. Rua Bahia was so pleasant back then, with its dairy stores and coffee shops. Avenida Afonso Pena was still lined with trees, but they all disappeared one day and I have no idea what explanation was given! There was an avenue circling the city. There was Alice's place. Then Pampulha emerged as an oasis in that beautiful provincial city.

I occasionally went to the Public Gardens to walk among the leafy trees and think about the theater that JK [Juscelino Kubitschek, the mayor of Belo Horizonte] wanted to build there, which has now been altered beyond recognition. I designed it with an entrance foyer opening onto the park. Access is now from the street, between the stores, as if such an inappropriate and inconceivable entrance could grace a theater. How easy it is, in Brazil, to interfere in other people's work and spoil it, with no respect for proper ethics!

This reminds me of the hotel in Ouro Preto, which I designed with great care and affection. It has been altered so that the *pilotis* are hemmed in by new construction and the building has been disfigured by furniture in incredibly bad taste. I recall the many times I tried to correct this work which was so poorly executed. I wrote my friend Israel Pinheiro, then governor of Minas Gerais, telling him I would not charge for the design for the Palace of Government building, asking him instead to use the money to repair the hotel in Ouro Preto. He was so moved that he had the letter framed and hung on the wall.

Some time afterward, Lúcio [Costa] called to tell me that the hotel was being destroyed, and I rushed to the site. The person in charge promised to fix the roof and carry out all the other unbelievable alterations that were required. The work was completed, but my design was totally altered by his innocent yet invariable lack of sensitivity. There was nothing I could do about it. Israel had tried to help me by ordering repairs at the hotel but had not realized that the person chosen to carry them out did not measure up to the task. Things are so different in the Old World! We still put up with such a lack of accountability here in Brazil!

Some years ago, in Paris, with the headquarters of the French Communist Party completed, Jacques Duclos, the general secretary of the FCP, called me to say, "Oscar, the building is ready and it is very beautiful, but I have a request to make. I have here an old desk, one with a history of its own, it has been with me all my life." He wanted to know if I would agree to place it in his new office. Now that is real consideration for people! True respect for the work of others! When shall we hear of this happening in Brazil?

I did a great deal of work with Le Corbusier. On the work for the United Nations building alone, we spent several months working together in New York. We used to talk every day and have lunch together, sharing our concerns and hopes as architects.

But our first contact was in 1936 in Rio, when, at the bidding of Lúcio [Costa], Gustavo Capanema, then minister of education, asked

Le Corbusier to give a series of lectures. Le Corbusier was struggling against the incomprehension that surrounded him professionally and was eager to prove his talent, so he quickly created two new works, the Ministry of Education and Health building and the University of Mangueira.

At that time we were somewhat removed from the core concerns of his architecture. We had read his exceptional work as if it were Holy Scripture, but, as it turned out, we were still not really in on all the details and secrets. This explained the masterly independence with which he quickly rejected Lúcio's U-shaped design for the ministry and adopted a different solution with the linear form that characterized most of his designs.

However, if I am to clarify his enthusiasm and the way he worked, I must go back and explain what really happened with his work in Rio. Having moved away from Lúcio's design, which he had used as the basic program, Le Corbusier drew up two plans: one for an ideal site near the ocean, the other for the downtown area that was ultimately chosen. This second design was then developed by the team I was on and that Lúcio directed.

As I saw it, the first plan was a much better one. When I saw the drawings being finished for the second design, I apprehensively attempted to bring in a different idea based on the first design. Carlos Leão liked my drafts and went to talk to Lúcio, but I had thrown the

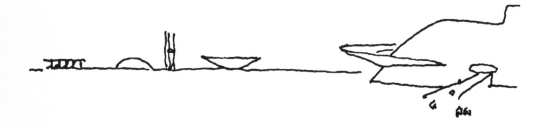

sketches out–it had never occurred me to that they might actually be used. Lúcio had us find them again, and they were approved. My layout had Le Corbusier's second design at the center of the site, with the great entrance hall opening on all sides onto the square, and with a more independent exhibition and auditorium space facing outward.

Since my collaboration in the design is frequently exaggerated or minimized, however, I can recall other suggestions I made, such as eliminating the extensions projected on the rear facade as a location for the bathrooms; adopting a central hallway instead of a uniform circulation pattern; and eliminating the first panel of the *brise-soleil* on the parapet.

I do remember that Jorge Moreira did not like my proposal. "Lúcio," he said, "the design is almost finished. Everything has been drafted." But Lúcio stuck to his opinion, and my suggestion was approved.

We should not forget that if it had not been for Lúcio, Le Corbusier's second design would have been built, and the facade would have been covered by vertical *brises*, like the Brazilian Press Association building, as I had gathered from some of the drawings and sketches.

When the design stage was concluded, we sent Le Corbusier a photo of the scale model. Unhappy at being considered the chief architect for the building, he drew a sketch on the photo and had it published in a Swiss magazine. The old master was going too far; our alterations, which appeared in that photo, were of little consequence in relation to his original concept.

We have always acknowledged the Ministry of Education design as being the work of Le Corbusier. On the commemorative plaque we wrote, "In accordance with the original sketch by Le Corbusier." In architectural vocabulary, the sketch is the original outline, the basic idea, the architectural invention.

My own architecture was to begin later, with my design for the Pampulha complex.

One day Gustavo Capanema took me to visit Minas Gerais governor Benedito Valadares, who was planning to build a casino in a remote suburban district of Belo Horizonte nicknamed *Acaba Mundo* (End of the World). On that occasion I met Juscelino "JK" Kubitschek, then a candidate for city mayor. I designed the project and showed it to Valadares, who then set the matter aside. Many months later the project was revived when JK summoned me to his office following his inauguration as city mayor.

On the scheduled date I went back to Belo Horizonte together with Rodrigo [M. F. de Andrade]. "I want to create a leisure district in Pampulha. I want to turn it into a lovely neighborhood, unlike anything in the entire country, with casino, club, church, and restaurant. By the way, I need the casino plans by tomorrow," JK told me. The next morning I handed him the plans, after having spent the night drawing in my room at the Central Hotel. I had never seen such great enthusiasm as I did in Kubitschek, such a strong desire for accomplishment, and such confidence surrounding an undertaking that, at that time, faced considerable obstacles.

The construction work began. JK followed its progress daily, convinced that the project would greatly benefit the city. I lose count of the many times we inspected the Pampulha site together! Time and again we went by motorboat to see the buildings reflected on the lake. JK could not contain his excitement. "How wonderful! This is going to be the most gorgeous neighborhood in the world!" he used to say. Indeed, the Pampulha project was a great challenge, particularly for JK, who had to seek impossible funding, fight the bureaucratic paralysis that surrounded him, and struggle against the provincial mentality of his peers.

Pampulha was the starting point of my career as an architect. I was totally enthusiastic about my first project, which also inaugurated a series of lengthy car trips on bumpy dirt roads, often so muddy that we were forced to stop for help. One day we even had a yoke of oxen towing our car! The project was an opportunity to challenge the monotony of contemporary architecture, the wave of misinterpreted functionalism that hindered it, and the dogmas of form and function that had emerged, counteracting the plastic freedom that reinforced concrete introduced. I was attracted by the curve–the liberated, sensual curve suggested by the possibilities of new technology yet so often recalled in venerable old baroque churches.

I take great pleasure in recollecting all the excitement stirred up by the construction of Pampulha. I particularly remember JK's zeal and the devotion of all who worked on the project. I also recall builder Ajax Rabello and his amiable nephew, Marco Paulo Rabello.[57] I met Rabello twenty years later in Brasília, at a time when he was once again collaborating with his friend JK, just like in the old days of the Pampulha project.

There the project stands today, defying its eternal antagonists. The small church with its harmonious, varied curves; the casino, the club, and the restaurant. The restaurant has open-air tables under a marquee that projects sinuously, as if to remind the viewer that well-designed and well-built curves can be beautiful, logical, and graceful.

Many people were favorably impressed by the Pampulha complex. Lúcio [Costa] went to see it, then sent me a telegram with his opinion: "Pampulha is a real beauty." Several years later, Jean de Roche, a colleague from Paris, made the following illuminating comment: "Pampulha was the great passion of my generation." Critics never tired of attacking it, but the wind was knocked out of their sails when the journal *Brazil Build* highlighted its architectural importance.

The criticisms did not bother me at all. I knew that someday critics would tire of their tedious sameness and start looking for something else. Now it is postmodernism they have turned to; they have accepted all the novelties they once rejected, only now these are a thousand times more conspicuous. Le Corbusier alone refused to jump on the bandwagon. I remember him once remarking, "Oscar, what you are doing is baroque, but it's very well done." And again, several years later, "They say my work is baroque, too. But just look at that photo of the model for the Congress of Chandigarh—not everyone could do that."

These very revealing comments complement another that I have selected from his friend Amédée Ozenfant's memoirs: "After so many years of purist discipline and loyalty to the right angle, Le Corbusier caught wind of the premise of a new baroque from elsewhere, and he seems to have decided to leave aside the honest right-angle, which he tended to regard as his private domain for so long. In the end, the baroque-born (Le Corbusier) does justice to himself—and as always with immense talent."[58]

During one of my trips to Paris, one of Le Corbusier's most discreet assistants made a somewhat sour remark about what was happening to the master's architecture; he felt Le Corbusier was lacking sensibility and passion. It was obvious that my architecture had influenced Le Corbusier's later projects, but this factor is only now being taken into account by critics of his work.

Here I am going to mention a dear old friend, a great engineer who worked with me for a long time. I see him in a photo that has yellowed with age: he is seated beside me on a park bench in Belo Horizonte. Joaquim Cardozo[59] gazes at the camera with a distant, ill-at-ease expression. He looks very thin, practically skin and bones.

I recall the many years we traveled around the world and to all parts of Brazil. I recall the countless subjects we discussed, the bitter pills we swallowed together in this absurd world. At times Cardozo would step out on the veranda in our office, look up at the sky, and declare, "We must get to the Observatory!" That would be the beginning of long conversations about the stars, infinite space, distant nebulae, and the grandeur of the universe. At other times we discussed literature. On those occasions Cardozo excitedly quoted Goethe from texts he had translated, or he recited his poem *Coronel de Macambira.*

More often than not our conversations revolved around our work, the relation between architecture and engineering, and the unfortunate misunderstanding of those who tried to work with reinforced concrete from the narrow viewpoint of rationalism that informed contemporary architecture. Amused, Cardozo promised to build solid-iron column bases as thin as I wished them to be.

We enjoyed reminiscing about our early days. We remembered the initial phase of construction of the Pampulha complex, and Kubitschek's enthusiastic remarks: "Oscar, this is going to be a beauty!" Smiling, we recalled the design for the church, which for so many years was rejected despite its simplicity, despite that it was enriched by paintings, decorative tiles, and the bas-reliefs by Candido Portinari, Ceschiatti, and Paulo Werneck.

We also discussed the jobs we undertook in Belo Horizonte, the events surrounding JK's tenure as state governor, the theater, library, public school, and yet another school named Escola Júlia Kubitschek. We talked about our frequent travels by car along muddy country roads or onboard old Central do Brasil railroad trains, their gentle to-and-fro movement often rocking us to sleep.

We spoke of Brasília and its impalpable dust, its hail-thunder-storms beating down on the tin roof of the wooden building used as a temporary presidential residence. We spoke of buildings rising out of that barren land that the city planner had so skillfully landscaped. Cardozo recollected the tremendous difficulty he faced designing the structure of the National Congress complex, and how enthusiastic he was the day he phoned me to say, "Oscar, I got the tangent that is going to allow the construction of a free-spanning dome for the House of Representatives, just like you want it!" Those were the good old days! Everything was like a dream–JK's favorite dream.

We never spoke about the accident at Gameleira,[60] which was so disgustingly exploited it deserves no comment. Certainly, however, we often thought about it and were revolted inside. My God, what terrible distress!

One day my friend Cardozo passed on, resentful of life and humankind. He was so thin he appeared as fragile as glass. I remember the day he phoned me from Recife, ill and upset: "Oscar, please send someone to get me." I promptly brought him to Rio, where I booked him a room near the office, at the Miramar Hotel. I picked him up every morning so he could spend the day with us. Although his memory was failing somewhat, Cardozo still smiled as he told his tales of Recife, the Gambrino Bar, and the old red-light district he enjoyed cruising "just for its local color!" as he would say.

In the evening I drove him back to the hotel and often joined him for dinner in his room. Actually, I felt bad about leaving him alone. He was a highly sensitive and solitary man who had become attached to me like someone who finds—and does not want to lose— his last friend in the world. From his chair in the drafting room, Cardozo closely followed the office routine. On occasion, if a visitor insisted on talking with me, he promptly interjected, taking the person by the elbow, as he did with Julio Niskier,[61] and saying, "All right, that's enough. Now you must let Oscar get back to work." However, Cardozo's illness advanced on its inexorable course, and after a while he could no longer stay at the hotel. I transferred him to the surgery ward of Casa de Saúde Eiras hospital, headed by my brother Paulo.

At the hospital, my friend was assigned a large room with three windows opening onto the garden. At first he seemed to be adapting well to that tranquil and comforting environment. He commented on the beautiful park, the mango trees loaded with fruit, the singing birds, and Dr. Metre, who came in for a daily visit. As his condition worsened, however, he grew irritable to the point that other patients, or even his own friends, greatly annoyed him. His daily routine included spending time outdoors, but gradually it became more difficult for him to return to his room. I remember one evening when he lay on the ground and refused to go inside. The physicians came out to help him. Cardozo told them, "I'm going to drown." One of the doctors gently replied, "Don't worry, Mr. Cardozo, there's no water here." In reply to which my friend, who never missed an opportunity to solve a technical problem, set his personal ordeal temporarily aside and advised, "Dig deep and you will find it." Two months later it was the hospital administration's turn to suggest that he be transferred—this time, to the psychiatric ward.

What a sad world! Where were all his friends who owed him consideration for his attention and reliable support? At a time of so much suffering, there were only five or six of us at his bedside.

Finally, one day I chartered a plane and flew Cardozo back to Recife, accompanied by his physician. Shortly afterward he died in a local hospital. My only consolation came from knowing that I had always treated him with affection from the bottom of my heart.

Many years earlier, I had become fully aware of my loyalty to Cardozo during a meeting in Brasília with the mayor Paulo de Tarso. "Mr. Niemeyer, I'm going to set up an expert commission to check Joaquim Cardozo's structural design for the Audit Court building," he told me. To which I promptly replied, "Cardozo is an old friend of mine. If you do this I will quit my position at city hall immediately." "In that case, send this survey form for him to fill out," de Tarso added, attempting conciliation. "I'll do so in your presence," I said. And I scribbled on the cover sheet, "Cardozo: Please fill out and return to this idiot." "You seem to have come straight from the Foreign Relations Department," the mayor said with a smile.

One day, at the office, Joaquim Cardozo made some remark that caused Estelita to protest: "That's not what you said yesterday." Cardozo was unrepentant and simply retorted, "Your job is to take note of what I say; I'll change my mind whenever I want to." We all laughed at Cardozo's nonchalant assertion of his right to switch

opinions. I kept quiet, but the incident reminded me of something similar in my own experience. On one occasion we had been standing beside the tall pillars of the Ministry of Education and Health building when Lúcio [Costa] observed, "Oscar, you said those columns were only four meters tall, but in fact they've always been ten meters tall." I remember my reaction of sheer disbelief, feeling sure that I was right.

Afterward, as I gave the subject more thought, I realized Lúcio was right. I was surprised and at the same time curious to learn what had led me to make such a mistake. Eventually I discovered what had happened. All the external columns of the building were in fact four meters tall as I had mentioned, but the interior columns, which I only partly saw from my vantage point behind the glass lobby wall, were indeed ten meters! It was a relief to discover how this metamorphosis had occurred. In removing the glass walls from the ground floor, exposing it to the plaza on all sides, I had given these interior columns fresh allure and more prominence. They were now free-floating and monumental. As Perret once observed, "One has to make the supports sing."[62] I felt that the modifications to Le Corbusier's original design had given the building a more free-flowing style; the columns had undeniably gained integrity, as people moved around them highlighting their scale and splendor.

I don't remember what caused Cardozo to change his mind that day, but I think he would have felt as much at ease to discuss it as I do now.

In 1947, Wallace Harrison asked me to join the team of architects commissioned with the design of the United Nations headquarters. On the very day I flew into New York, Le Corbusier rang me at my hotel and asked me to meet him on a corner of Fifth Avenue.

It was cold outside, so Harrison considerately draped his own coat over mine, saying, "I'll do as Saint Francis did." Then, as we walked to Oscar Nitzke's[63] home a few blocks away, he told me about the UN job. His design was being criticized and he wanted me to work with him on the project. I agreed to his request, and for several days I did my best to help him.

One day, however, Harrison summoned me to his office. "Oscar, I haven't brought you here to collaborate with Le Corbusier. I have brought you here to contribute your own design, like the other architects." The moment Le Corbusier learned about this he replied,

"You can't do that, it would only lead to confusion." Nonetheless, a few days later, he advised me, "You'd better do it. They're expecting a design from you." I had my draft plan ready in a week. I must admit, I did not like Le Corbusier's scheme; it seemed destined for a different site. The tower he devised for the General Assembly and the Conference Building split the site awkwardly in two.

In my scheme, I kept the indispensable Secretariat block but separated the General Assembly from the Conference Building, placing the latter in a long block by the river and the former at the edge of the site. That was how the United Nations Plaza came to be created.

Budiansky,[64] who at the time was Le Corbusier's assistant, was the first person to see it. "Yours is better than his!" was his reaction. Le Corbusier then came in and slowly scrutinized it before commenting, "That is one elegant design!"

Once again Wallace Harrison called me to his office. "Oscar, we all favor your scheme; I'm going to put it forward at the next meeting." So he did. On the day of the meeting, I rode the elevator with the architect representing China, who told me, "Today, I am on your side." Before the meeting began, Le Corbusier again tried to argue for his design: "My drawings may not be so pretty, but this is the scientific solution to the whole program of the United Nations." I realized that he was referring to my design.

The meeting started and Wallace Harrison presented my scheme, which was unanimously accepted. The attendees congratulated me, and even the secretary embraced me. My project had been selected. On the way out, Le Corbusier murmured, "I'd like to see you tomorrow morning."

The next morning I went to meet him. He wanted to relocate the General Assembly to the center of the site. "This is the most important part of the hierarchy, and that is the right place for it," he said. I did not agree, since this would do away with the United Nations Plaza and split the site in two again. But Le Corbusier was so adamant, and he seemed so concerned, that I ended up agreeing. Together we presented a new plan, referred to as Scheme 23A–32 (23A was his project number and 32 was mine).

Wallace Harrison was not keen on this option. After all, we had already agreed on the plan, so the work proceeded with the introduction of minor changes. Ultimately, the constructed complex featured the free volumes and spaces of Scheme 23A–32. The final result, however, was produced by teamwork; our task had only been to decide on the architectural parti. The actual plans and their details were drawn up by Wallace Harrison, Max Abramovitz,[65] and their assistants. That is the way I remember the episode. As far as Wallace Harrison and Abramovitz were concerned, my memories are of their cordial politeness and friendship.

As for Le Corbusier, he never liked to talk about Scheme 23A–32, but I do remember him many years later, at lunch in his apartment, staring at me for some time before saying, "You are so generous." I felt that he was remembering that morning in New York, somewhat belatedly no doubt, when for his sake I had put aside my own project, which had already been selected by the architects' committee.

It would be natural, in light of the episode I have described, for me to speak of Le Corbusier in a less friendly manner. But this is not the case. I remember him today with the same enthusiasm I felt the first time we met, forty years ago, when we went to pick him up at the airport. He seemed to be an architect-genius come down from heaven. If, on the one hand, he was sometimes overly eager to make his own architecture, on the other hand I always felt he was a human being who carried a message, a paean to beauty that could not be silenced. Accept and understand him: that is what I always tried to do.

In 1950, Juscelino Kubitschek was elected governor of the state of Minas Gerais. Pampulha had just been finished, and it turned out to be, as he predicted, the city's newest and most elegant neighborhood, with its floodlit casino, lights reflecting in the reservoir waters, and the local bourgeoisie parading in the midst of its marble, mirrors, and onyx.

JK selected me for all the subsequent jobs that came up; I had become his favorite architect. He was now commissioning works all over the state. In Belo Horizonte, I designed the restoration of his residence, Casa das Mangabeiras; the library; a public school; the theater—which was later totally ruined by a remodel; the Banco da Produção in the city of Juiz de Fora; the Banco do Brasil building in Diamantina, JK's home town, where I also designed the club, school, and hotel.

Time went by and JK was elected to the National Congress. Soon after that he became President of Brazil and immediately looked me up. He came to my home at Canoas and eagerly told me of his plans as we drove back to the city together: "I am going to build a new capital for this country and I want you to help me." He still had that same enthusiasm of twenty years before. "Oscar, this time we are going to build the capital of Brazil. A modern capital, the most beautiful capital in the world!"

From that moment on, the idea of Brasília dominated our conversations. At his request, I talked to Israel Pinheiro, who was charged with overseeing the actual construction work, and a few days later I was on a plane with JK and his entourage, flying over the chosen site.

It was a huge and dismal patch of wilderness in the remote central interior plain. But to my surprise, my doubts crumbled away in the face of his optimism. Everything about him was so clear and transparent, his vision and determination were so contagious, that I was soon persuaded that in a couple of years our country's new capital would rise up from this place at the farthest reaches of the earth. JK was as motivated as he had been years before when he built Pampulha. He couldn't wait. "Let's get started with the government building and the hotel!" he said.

The first thing I had to build in those bare backlands was a base camp for him, somewhere he could stay on his weekend inspection visits. The matter was resolved at Juca's Bar, with Milton Prates.[66] I designed a house made of wood: on the first floor there was a living room, bedrooms, and bathrooms; on the ground floor, the kitchen and dining area. I got a bank loan to build it and within ten days the house was ready. It was a present for JK and was named "Catetinho."[67]

The blueprints for Brasília were being drawn up in the Ministry of Education and Health building. We soon realized that they should be done on site, along with the follow-up on the work already underway, so we sped up the construction of the modest public housing where we were to stay.

Before going to Brasília, I talked to Israel Pinheiro and made a list of people whom he should send to join me, agreed on their salaries, and so forth. He told me about my own design contract. I was to earn the usual salary for public employees, but he added, "I can pay you a commission." I immediately refused: "Forget the commission." I have always detested this word. Perhaps I would have accepted if he had put it another way and had said something like, "Your salary will be so-much, but you will also get a percentage of the total value, as regulated by the Institute of Architects of Brazil." So it was on account of rejecting the word "commission" that I drew up all the plans for Brasília for only forty thousand cruzeiros a month.[68]

The money issue did not bother me at all. In fact, the experience did me good. Because I was earning so little and had practically shut down my office in Rio, I felt no qualms about doing the job my way. The greatest joy of all was hiring whomever I wanted to work with me on the new capital. That's why I summoned lots of friends: first, about twenty architects for the planned projects; then various friends from different professions, whom I hired for the simple pleasure of helping them out, since I knew they were short of money. As it turned out, our team included a physician, a journalist, a lawyer, a goalkeeper from the Flamengo soccer team, and others of even more dubious professional classification. They were all useful to me, and the team became more flexible, the conversation more versatile, the work more complete, with each member contributing according to his own area of specialty.

We soon formed a cohesive and friendly group as we moved into the modest houses that were being built. They were far from luxurious–just a living room, two bedrooms, bathroom, and kitchen. In my small room I had a cot, a small wardrobe, and a stool for a bedside table. The area all around us was empty land, unprotected, covered in dust during the winter, and water and mud during the summer.

Of course, we hardly noticed the lack of comfort, since we were so intensely involved in our work. But there was that feeling of being at the end of the world, missing far-off family and friends, cut off from roads and telephones. A little field radio was all we had for entertainment. It was worse for those who were single, imagining how good it would be to have a wife at their side to share their woes and affection. The solitude gave rise to many surreptitious liaisons.

For diversion we got together at night to chat, discuss the ongoing work, play cards, and later on to make our own music with Paulão on the guitar, Sabino on the tambourine, and me trying hard to keep up on my little *cavaquinho*.[59] Other friends sang along, and Willy, who had samba in his bones, danced all around us with a wonderful sense of rhythm.

Sometimes we would go to the new capital's "wild west"–a stretch known as Cidade Livre (Free City), a long, mud-covered road packed with jeeps, horses, and carts, lined with low brick buildings housing stores, bars, restaurants, clubs, and the local prostitutes. We would sit in a club and happily watch the social mixing taking place in this forsaken backwater. The liquor flowed while our colleagues–the architects, engineers, and construction workers–danced all together around the wooden-plank floor. There was a mood of nostalgia for home and the distant places where these men had come from to work together in Brasília.

The construction work progressed. Red dust settled on new streets and the noise and bustle of the construction sites filled the air as the city began to welcome its first real inhabitants.

JK was determined to stay on schedule, and he was the first to set an example, ignoring the criticism of the reactionaries who sought to derail the endeavor. He laughed at those who said the location was wrong, that neither gardens nor vegetation would grow there, that the water of the lake we designed would be absorbed by the porous soil. But we stayed on schedule, and Israel, JK's right-hand man, managed the site without hesitation or red tape. He demonstrated the spirit that only people who know they are doing the right thing possess. I worked from dawn to dusk and toured the works until late at night with JK. There was no time to lose. No sooner were the foundations for a building drafted than work would start. The rest of the details and structures followed the construction schedule.

JK's vision–and mine, too–was not one of a backward provincial city, but of a modern and up-to-date city, one that would represent the importance of our country.

Niemeyer (far left) with Jean-Paul Sartre (second from left), Brasília, 1959

Niemeyer (right) in his office with Luis Carlos Prestes, Rio de Janeiro, 1970s

Niemeyer (right) with Darcy Ribeiro, 1980s

Niemeyer (seated, far right) in his office with Fidel Castro, Rio de Janeiro, 1992

Niemeyer with his father, late 1940s

Some nights JK would ask us around to the presidential residence. He was alone in Brasília, without any family there, and he enjoyed having guests, so we went over–Milton Prates, César Prates, Rochinha, Juca Chaves, Bené Nunes, Dilermano Reis[70] with his guitar, and me. Some of them brought company along. Some went alone, as I did. In the rooms of the country's presidential residence, we sat in a circle around JK and listened to his yarns.

The subject matter was always the same: the obstacles we faced, slander campaigns, economic and political problems, JK's obstinant desire to finish everything on schedule. He questioned us about details he had been unaware of in relation to people trying to hold up the work in Brasília, and he would conclude bitterly: "Those bastards!" We would listen attentively to his passionate speeches, happy to see him so confident and optimistic. He renewed his faith in his vision and chatted in confidence among friends. It was good for him, and even better for us, as concerned as we were with the future of the project.

Dilermano's old-time waltzes provided the musical backdrop and César Prates hollered out sentimental Brazilian songs from the past. Bené sat at the piano and played his varied repertoire. Occasionally he played one of JK's favorite samba tunes, and the president would dance jovially and uninhibitedly, happy to set aside his worries for a few precious moments.

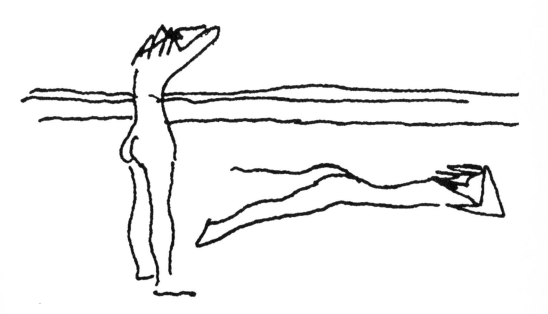

Then the party resumed the conversation: Brasilia and the schedules, or the new Belém-Brasília highway–the mighty attempt to build this road, the felling of forests, the gigantic trees, the crossing of rivers, hills, and swampland of the ancient, mysterious, and unknown Amazon region.

And so, that is how we spent those unforgettable evenings which left behind memories of a president who had tremendous dynamism for his work but still knew how to take the time to see his friends, to laugh and have a little fun like anybody else.

It was usually very late, past one o'clock in the morning, when JK walked us out to our cars. And we would linger there, enraptured by the immense, star-studded sky of Brasília and by the government buildings standing high and white against the dark brushlands all around. JK would take my arm and say gently, as if confiding a secret, "Niemeyer, this is gorgeous!"

My work in Brasília required making long journeys by car along unfinished highways worse than anything I had seen before. Over twelve-hundred kilometers of mud or clouds of red dust from the brushlands separated Rio from Brasília.

One time we were driving a Saab, and Brasília was still a good six-hundred kilometers away. The car was cruising along just fine and the weather was splendid. I was taking turns at the wheel with Gadelha[7] while Galdino Duprat and Eça lounged in the back seat. Duprat was furious because he had gotten into the car thinking he was headed for Belo Horizonte, and here he was on the way to Brasília. From time to time we stopped for a rest. When it was time to go, Gadelha politely held the door open and said, "Get in, Duprat!" Now Duprat, who hated to take orders, invariably rejected this courtesy and yelled back, "I'm not getting in. You think you're a Brazilian Communist Party organizer with your 'Get in Duprat' and your 'Get out Duprat.'" Then we all burst out laughing as our old friend showed his teeth again.

We got back on the road under a clear sky and a bracing wind. The low, sparse vegetation was monotonously repetitive, and the dry and stunted trees seemed to strain up from the ground as if resisting the soil's attempts to pull them back down into the earth. After several hours' driving, we reached the river and got out to stretch our legs and wait for the ferryboat man to appear. Those trips to Brasília were really exhausting. As in Pampulha, the new highway was only paved after the city was built. So there we were, tired and spent as we waited for the ferry.

The journey continued. The road began to seem unfamiliar. The vegetation was so dense and the roadway so bad that something odd was bound to happen–and it did. We felt a strong jolt and the car suddenly stopped. We had driven into a huge pothole. Forgetting that we were on a slope, we pushed the Saab back onto the road, where it rolled downhill, out of control. We ran after it, trying to stop it, looking like the Three Stooges. The Saab rolled into the brush, and we listlessly got around to figuring how to hoist it out. The brush was shoulder-height, but there was nothing we could do except start pushing and pulling. The ground was riddled with holes, however, and Duprat was the first to fall into one of them. "Get me out of here, I'm hurt!" he yelled. We pulled him out and then, after much straining, got the car out, too.

The engine roared to life, no problems there. The journey proceeded without further incident until the car petered to a halt on a steep incline. Second gear would not engage. We tried everything, gunning the engine and tugging at the stick shift. My friends got out to see if a lighter load would help, but it was no use. We were stuck again.

We had no idea where we were. The night was pitch black and the slightest noise was amplified against the vast silence around us.

Duprat was frightened and asked, "Are there Indians around here?" Eça tried to scare him: "Sure to be. We're in the heart of the backlands here, far from anywhere. Must have taken a wrong turn onto an abandoned road." In fact, we were feeling somewhat lost and forlorn in the middle of nowhere.

Night closed in. Absolute darkness. It was two or three o'clock in the morning and not a single vehicle had come our way. The cold pierced our bones, so we huddled together to keep warm. Nobody could get any sleep. "Oh, shit!" From deep in the bush, there appeared two points of light, and the usual jokes began. "Must be a jaguar!" said Eça ironically. But Duprat was taking it seriously: "Just might be one!" We peered into the dark, curious to see how Duprat would react. But one of the points of light suddenly went out. "That's no jaguar!" blurted a relieved Duprat. But Eça wasn't giving up: "Must be a cockeyed cat." Duprat was provoked and he retorted, "Cockeyed was the slut who gave birth to you. . ." So that was the way we spent the night, telling tall tales and ragging Duprat. It was just the escape we needed on that endless and weary night.

Daybreak arrived, heralded by a blood-red sky and streaks of light piercing through the trees. The brushlands awoke, birds sang, life pulsated everywhere around us. Could it be that we had lost our way and were far from the right road? Around nine o'clock a truck appeared on the horizon. Gadelha and I hopped on, perched on the sacks, and jolted off down the endless road to seek help.

The administrations of Jânio Quadros and João "Jango" Goulart[2] were followed by dark days of dictatorship as reactionaries seized power with the support of U.S. imperialist policy. Jânio Quadros wrote an inopportune letter of resignation, and this was the pretext they needed to get rid of him. His progressive foreign policy, his support for developing communities and underprivileged peoples, and his response to the pretensions of the U.S. State Department were the real reasons for what came next.

Vice President Jango assumed the Brazilian presidency and continued to take a progressive line. The masses held huge street demonstrations as the left enjoyed freedom of movement; as a result, the same people who had removed Quadros from office targeted Jango, too.

Then came the military coup and the dictatorship that ruled the country during twenty years of oppression. Those who fought heroically for freedom and democracy were tortured and killed. In those days there was no deliberate attempt to disfigure the new capital city; it was simply neglected or ignored. Consequently, badly designed buildings and ugly architecture crept in and ruined the visual unity we had hoped to preserve in Brasília.

I was in Europe when the coup took place and when the police searched my office and the headquarters of the journal *Módulo*. The day after my return to Brazil at the end of 1964, I was taken to army barracks for questioning. I admitted to having written in a Soviet magazine that I supported Cuba and all the underdeveloped peoples of Asia, Africa, and the Americas. Two days later I gave an interview to the weekly magazine *Manchete*. I told the reporter, "Ask me who my best friends are." And I went on, "Luís Carlos Prestes, Juscelino Kubitschek, Darcy Ribeiro, and Marcos Jaymovitch.[73] I am naming them because, as well as being my friends, they are the underdogs now, and this is when friends have to show their faces." I was disgusted by the complicit silence that hung over them.

My life went on without any major problems. I was the architect responsible for Brasília and–as everybody knew–I had worked there since the beginning, honestly, without a break, for next to nothing. I was a member of the steering committee appointed by Congress to oversee the new city's urban planning and architecture, along with Israel Pinheiro and Lúcio Costa.

The government yielded to pressure from the most reactionary elements, but not Congress, or the Senate, or the House. I received full support from Gilberto Marinho and Petrônio Portela in the Senate, and from José Bonifácio, Pereira Lopes, and Marco Maciel in the House. Not to mention the friendship of Luciano Brandão, director-general of the House of Representatives.

It was during the Médici government, however, that the reactionaries decided to put an end to my work as an architect. Problems began when my design for the new airport terminal in Brasília was turned down because it was circular. Brigadier Henrique Castro Neves, director of engineering at the Air Force Ministry, attempted to explain: "In the future we will need to build extensions to the airport." Their outdated solution, a rectangular shape, should have been rejected. The circular design was the right one. That is why, years later, Charles De Gaulle airport in Paris was built in a circular shape. Even in Brazil, the same people who had criticized me had a circular terminal built at Rio's Galeão International Airport.

I was indignant and determined to protest. Lacking in arguments but holding power, the Air Force Ministry placed a plaque on the work reading "Military Airport." Again I went to the newspapers to say that this was a lie, since military airports had no stores, customs checks, or restaurants. I took the matter to court with a class-action suit against the Air Force Ministry. The case was lost and a judge from Belo Horizonte–what a bastard he was!–preposterously ruled that I should pay the trial costs of nearly six million cruzeiros. So there it is, dear reader–an obsolete airport, lacking architectural unity, and tarnishing the main port of entry to the new capital. It was a fierce struggle on both sides, polarized left and right. The right was strengthened by the outcome of the court case and began to persecute me more openly. We were now living under a no-holds-barred fascist government headed by Médici.

My work began to be rejected and I was threatened with dismissal from my job. This was the second attempt to fire me. The first, in 1964, had been thwarted by mayor General Ivan Souza,[74] who refused to sign the order. The political police questioned me several times. Even during the JK government, at the height of the construction of Brasília, they had called me in for questioning. The pressure was on. The police stormed the university, colleagues were expelled–almost two hundred faculty members–and I resigned in protest against such brutality. Ultimately it was not these threats that were most repulsive but the hostility orchestrated by Colonel Manso Neto.[75] The whole thing was too disgusting for words.

I decided to pack up my architecture and my hurt feelings and go abroad. Those who were trying to blackball me, without realizing it, had presented me with the greatest opportunity of my life: to practice my trade as an architect in the Old World and to have them learn to appreciate my nimble forms and curves.

I spent a long time traveling around Europe, visiting Brazil often but quickly returning to my works in progress. The news from Brazil was not good: arrests and torture, and the dictatorship continuing with its ignoble task. I was in Paris, and the bad news plunged us into a mood of unbearable pessimism. One day we decided to do something to fight this mood. Friends called an actress we knew, and we held a small party in the office after hours.

We had done the same thing back in Brasília to welcome foreign architects on the jury for the public competition organized to select a design for the city's master plan (known as the Plano Piloto). "None of your snooty cocktail parties," Mário Catrambi[76] had said. "When a man wants to party, he needs a woman. Let's call up a few girls." We amused ourselves thinking about how our cool and collected guest, Sir William Halford,[77] would tell his colleagues of the special welcome he had been given. Would he have had a story to tell if we had done the opposite and held a boring social affair, dripping with lies and hypocrisy?

We had gotten together at Mário's house, in Leme. There were the four jury members, six women, and my friends Di, Ari Barroso,[78] Hélio Uchôa, and Gauss Estelita. What fun everybody had! Mário had warned us right away: "Nobody goes out to the garden without their clothes on." So the party was confined to the living room and the bedrooms. It was the cordial, all-too-human kind of event that only the surrealists of Paris could have conceived.

I remember Di sketching the visitors; Mário laughing, drinks in hand; William Halford hugging one of the girls; Sive[79] with another. . . .It was a meeting of uninhibited men, full of joie de vivre, out to have a great time. The party did not stop us from earnestly examining the designs the next day as we collected submissions for the Plano Piloto. We were concerned to keep the competition honest and select the best piece of work.

I became friends with William Halford, and I remember that when he returned on his second trip to Brazil he was euphoric every time he recalled that party. His contact with us had left him with an impression of Brazilians that went beyond the stereotypical image of friendly, uncomplicated people. He saw us instead as normal human beings, living life to its fullest as we should do, with all its pleasures and sorrows. I can still see him now, affectionately patting me on the shoulder and saying, "Oscar, what a delight it was to meet you and your friends! So warm, humble, and genuine, as everyone should be."

As soon as I reached Paris, at the end of 1964, Heron de Alencar[80] came to see me; he was a dear old friend from the University of Brasília. The following day he brought along Miguel Arraes,[81] who wanted to discuss the situation in Brazil and the revolt he was organizing. He told me he had six thousand armed men in Pernambuco, and he asked me to join the revolution as secretary and design an emblem for it; he sent me a book of symbols the next day. Of course, the whole affair was forgotten and we heard no more from Arraes, whom I came across later in Algeria. He settled there and lived a trouble-free life in that country. He was a strange and cautious man, but his political positions were consistent.

For several years, Heron de Alencar, Luis Hildebrando, Ubirajara Brito, and Euvaldo Mattos[82] came to my Paris apartment every night and we played cards, chatted, or went out to a neighborhood bar to discuss things over a drink. Occasionally the conversation touched on cultural issues and cultural leaders in Brazil. But we were so wrapped up in the political struggle, so involved in the dramatic situation facing our comrades and brothers, that we had no time for anything that was not somehow related to solidarity or revolt. Our nights went by, identical and pointless, and all we talked of was this constant concern. It was only when something more serious happened, or some comrade traveling incognito contacted us, that our little group expanded and the conversation switched to other subjects.

L'Humanité, the French Communist Party newspaper, held a festival every September and this brought us a fresh breeze of hope and enthusiasm. Luiz Hildebrando was in charge of organizing the Brazilian party's stand, and the well-worn, optimistic phrases would be dusted off: "Victory will be ours," "Time is on our side," "Capitalism is dying." And we would laugh and feel confident about the future of this age-old struggle against injustice. Those were wonderful events: three days of festivities, with thousands of people embracing each other in solidarity and browsing the stands as if a brave new world was already beginning! My first festival there was such a pleasant surprise! I had never seen anything like it anywhere, such a festive and spontaneous mood of love and fraternity. It was as if an enormous family of good and honorable people, without pretensions whatsoever, had come together to prove that someday life will be better and happier.

I cannot tell you that my Brazilian Communist Party membership brought me only joy, enhanced knowledge, and the unwavering posture of a leftist which I have always assumed and never denied. This political association also brought multiple hardships to my career over the years. It is obvious that nothing I endured compares with the sacrifice of many party members who were locked up, tortured, and killed by reactionary forces. However, on a lesser scale, of course, I did pay a price for my political beliefs. I cannot remember dates, but I will try to list in chronological order some of the minor problems I experienced, although I have already mentioned some of them.

When the political police called me in for questioning, they took me around to the different departments and showed the staff my face, saying, "This is Oscar Niemeyer, the architect." This was their way of "putting me on file," as they later told me.

On one occasion, I was at the UN when I heard I had just won, in Rio, a competition for the National Aeronautic Center. But then I received a telegram advising me that the award had been annulled. I protested, but my lawyer, Evandro Lins e Silva,[85] reported, "There's nothing we can do. They are alleging that it's for national security reasons."

On another occasion, I was invited to join the São Paulo University School of Architecture (FAU/USP) faculty in São Paulo when an objection was raised. The students went on strike in retaliation against the most reactionary council member, Ernesto Leme.

Then I was invited to teach at Yale, but my visa application was denied; this went on for several years. Once when I was in Rome, I was again invited to the United States, so I applied for a visa at the local U.S. embassy. Yet again, I was denied entry into the country, and I declared, "You know, I'm quite pleased with this. If you continue to refuse me a visa after twenty years, it means I haven't changed!"

A few years later, a U.S. citizen of high status extended me an invitation. I got a two-week permit for myself and a six-month permit for my companion, Carlos Magalhães da Silveira.[84] We went to New York and visited the United Nations, where I told reporters, "I am happy to be able to visit this building, to which I made a contribution as an architect, and I am even happier to learn that Communist China is being admitted to the UN today." To which my American host commented, "There goes your visa extension!" I left the country two weeks later.

I was called in again by the political police as work was starting on Brasília. I reported the fact to JK [Juscelino Kubitschek], who responded, "You can't go in there. They'll take your photo and I won't be able to invite you to the official residence." He picked up the phone in front of me and called General Kruel.[85] "I can't have Niemeyer being questioned by the political police. He's my key man in Brasília." In spite of this order, I was, in fact, called in for questioning the following month. The interrogation room had padded walls. There were the usual questions about the Brazilian Communist Party and so forth. Finally they asked, "What is it that you guys want?" I replied: "To change society." "Take that down," said the police officer to the *negrinho*[86] who was typing up the interview: "'To change society.'" The typist turned toward me and remarked, "Now that's going to be difficult." What ignorance!

In 1964, while I was living abroad, the police searched my offices and those of the journal *Módulo*. Mauro Vinhas was so terror-stricken that he committed suicide. At the end of that year I returned to Brazil. My daughter was a friend of Castelo Branco's[87] daughter, who had wanted to intercede in my favor, but I had written back telling her not to do so. The day after my arrival in Rio, I was taken to army barracks. On the balcony overlooking the courtyard, I met Astrojildo Pereira,[88] who was a prisoner there. We embraced each other with great emotion.

In the interrogation room, the officer asked me several questions:

"Do you write for a Soviet magazine?"

"Yes."

"Have you supported Cuba in articles and manifestos?"

"Yes, Cuba and all underdeveloped countries of Africa, Asia, and the Americas."

More questions followed and then, as I was leaving, the officer, who had been surprisingly polite, remarked, "I'm sorry we had to meet under such unpleasant circumstances." Then he asked, "Would you like to visit your friend?" I accepted the offer and spent some time chatting to Astrojildo in his cell.

The students at the University of Juiz de Fora asked me to lecture there, but when I arrived the dean refused to let me in. The lecture had to be held at another venue.

The first mayor of Brasília after the 1964 coup was General Ivan Souza Mendes, and he was under pressure to fire me for being a Communist, but he refused to do so. Just a few days ago, he told me what had happened.

The mayor of Brasília during the Médici administration was a fool and President Médici himself was a reactionary. They tried to have me fired. They asked me to submit designs for projects only to turn them down when they were ready. I felt like leaving.

While I was abroad, I learned that Gustavo Capanema had called on the mayor to argue in my favor. Nobody else did so. I was reminded of the time when, for much less, I myself had threatened to leave Brasília in defense of Joaquim Cardozo.

This wretched affair became ridiculous when Colonel Manso Neto falsified some design drafts in an attempt to prove that I was copying Le Corbusier. He showed them to my friend and colleague Birunga,[89] who protested, "This is ridiculous!" But the plot went ahead and copies of these drafts were made at city hall and shown to

ministers and top government officials. I only learned of the details of this outrageous affair some time later and, unable to get hold of a copy of the drafts, I could not respond. I gave interviews to denounce the plot and Colonel Manso, who had acted in such disgraceful manner.

I never kept quiet about anything. I have never concealed my political position as a Communist. The more understanding individuals who commission me as an architect are well aware of my ideological status. They believe I am mistaken, and I believe they are mistaken.

The journal *Módulo* was one of the sidelines that kept me busy and amused. Our original idea had been to publish a review following definite editorial principles, rather than just another architecture compendium. Keeping it going, however, was truly hard work. Working against it was the Brazilian tendency to shun this kind of advocacy, especially given the leftist political positions of those collaborating on the journal. It was only during the period of Brasília's construction that *Módulo* made some headway. We were rooting for JK and his project for a new capital, which was enduring stiff resistance from the opposition.

But then came the military coup in 1964; the editorial offices were searched and the publication plunged into a long period of difficulties. To begin, Gadelha was arrested. Marcos Jaymovitch, who was accused of being a "Soviet spy," went into exile. Mauro Vinhas, who had been arrested several years earlier during a nationalist campaign to keep the oil industry in Brazilian hands (under the slogan *O petróleo é nosso* [The Oil is Ours]), grew so indignant that he committed suicide. I myself was abroad, but even so, the "cops," under reactionary orders, searched my office. The journal began to experience trouble as advertisers dropped out–some on account of the expenses involved, others because they were utter reactionaries themselves.

Nevertheless, the journal inspired the unflagging enthusiasm of Maria Luíza, Marcus Lontra, and Vera Lúcia,[90] who at a certain point took over the editorial work and attempted to keep the publication going at great personal sacrifice. I am greatly indebted to them for their absolute commitment, and even though *Módulo* is, to this day, not a regular publication, it did give Marcus the opportunity to become part of the art world, where he is now an accomplished and talented figure.

In Paris, the special events sponsored by *L'Humanité* featured display booths, snack bars, restaurants, playgrounds, shows, theater performances, art exhibitions, and the party's message delivered to an assemblage bursting with confidence and determination. At one of these festivals, the party comrades asked me to design a huge stage for a Soviet ballet performance. It had to be a portable, covered stage, some twenty meters long and easy to assemble. I suggested four bulldozers that would support a canvas cover with their blades, with steel cables supporting wooden planks. The party leased the bulldozers, built the stage and its cover as I had suggested, and put on the great spectacle. It was a tremendous feeling when I saw the whole thing set up, with the huge red canvas that seemed to hover in the air above the stage!

I just loved the Paris of Gide, Baudelaire, Malraux, and Camus, with its memories of revolution and liberty. The ancient Seine flowed stoically through the city, unconcerned with us humans and our humdrum lives. There was the Champs Elysées and its sidewalks, the cafés, glamorous store windows, and gorgeous girls. Paris for me was also the boulevard Raspail, where I later lived. All the buildings there were of matching height, with high windows and flower-bedecked balconies. This was the Paris of Sartre and Simone de Beauvoir, Aragon, and Nizan.[91]

How I loved roaming the Parisian streets and getting to know the city better, or just sitting at La Coupole, sipping a glass of wine. . . . The Paris of royal palaces, the great Boulogne and Fontainebleau parks, the Left Bank; the stomping ground of Fitzgerald, Hemingway, Gris, and Cocteau; the home of La Rotonde, Flore, and Deux Magots.

I remember once meeting Jean-Paul Sartre in Brasília. We were standing before the presidential office building, Palácio do Planalto, when he remarked, "How beautiful it is! Its columns seem to embrace us like a fan!" One day, in Paris, he phoned me with an invitation to attend a political demonstration. But Gosnat,[92] my friend from the French Communist Party, was against it, and advised, "You shouldn't go. They never invite us." So I did not go, but I sent a sympathetic message that was read from the platform.

I admired Sartre's intelligence, his consistent position in defense of underprivileged peoples, his spirit of rebellion against bourgeois dogmas and prejudices–although at times he went overboard. I once read in a book, "Sartre turned up naked for a party, and Nizan was almost naked too." This kind of behavior would have been considered scandalous in Brazil, but it was not shocking in France, which was then experiencing the height of Surrealism. And wholesale defiance was the aim of Surrealism at that time, with Breton, Buñuel, Aragon, and several others meeting at the Cyrano café in Pigalle to discuss their strategies in the struggle against society, in which scandalous behavior often figured as the appropriate solution. But all that was long before Sartre came up with his idea of existentialism, which for several years made him a leader for a great many young people in France.

I am indebted to André Malraux for assisting me with my work in France and for his interest in my architecture; thanks to his intervention I became architect for the town of Grasse. I remember him visiting my exhibition, and his constant appreciation. "Oscar, your architecture is part of my imaginary museum. That is where I keep all that I have seen and loved in this world."

I greatly admired his intelligence and the well-informed and scintillating ease with which he darted from one issue to another. I read his complete work, from *La Condition humaine* to *Antimémoires* and *Les Chênes qu'on abat*. It was wonderful to talk or just listen to him, a learned individual who could turn his mind to anything!

Raymond Aron[93] was another personality I was fortunate to meet, although we disagreed politically. He was chosen to sponsor my nomination for the Collège de France and invited me to dinner several times. Aron was eager to get to know me. The last time we met he said, "Good. Now you just have to look up the Collège secretary and schedule the required interviews." This procedure was the same as that adopted by the Academy of Letters in Rio, so I decided to drop the issue altogether. Several months later he wrote me a letter deploring the fact.

I met Aragon several times and even went to visit him in the hospital with Claude Leroy.[94] He was polite, amiable, and intelligent, a great poet and comrade. I was always surprised to find that with all his refinement and sensitivity, Aragon had been part of the same Surrealist group as Buñuel, Dali, and the others in all their exploits around the city. I even got to meet Jean Genet.[95] I remember the day we had lunch at La Coupole, and my surprise at his easygoing appearance and his serene and smiling personality.

One day, British novelist Graham Greene telephoned me in Paris. "Niemeyer, we belong to this important organization called the American Academy of Arts and Sciences. They are refusing to protest against American interventionism around the world, so I'm organizing a group to resign from it. Will you join us?" I agreed to resign, of course.

I have always felt ill at ease among these associations of intellectuals who discuss everything except the major political issues that impact on humanity. This is one of my reasons for not joining that sort of organization.

After Paris, Algiers was the foreign city where I spent the most time. I particularly liked the city, the readily apparent support it showed for Dejelloul, and the special consideration President Boumedienne[96] showed for me. I loved the friendly streets winding down to the seafront; the inlets, coves, and pebble beaches of the old Mediterranean, full of legends and mysteries; the tiny, white, almost windowless houses huddling against the winds. And I loved the Casbah, with the terrible rattle of women banging pots to warn the occupying forces that colonialism was coming to an end.

It was in Constantine, however, that I executed one of my best projects, the University of Constantine campus. I was reluctant to create just another university campus; rather, I wanted this one to reflect contemporary architectural practice and, as I have mentioned before, to show the world how far Brazilian engineering had progressed. So I designed the Bâtiment de Classes, a building supported on *pilotis* with fifty-meter spans and twenty-five-meter cantilevers.

As usual, the technical bureau in Algiers reviewed our design, and their judgment was that the facade—which was virtually a large, longitudinal girder—would have to be one and a half meters thick! But Bruno Contarini, my engineer, proved to them that our design was accurate, so he built a wall that was just thirty centimeters thick. The other buildings also followed this structurally exacting design, including the auditorium, where we adopted a new solution with an exposed girder and two supporting wings that added audacity to the structure. We were beginning to show the Old World that there wasn't much they could teach us Latin Americans.

This concern for innovative creativity was maintained when we examined the program and rejected the initial idea of an ordinary university complex with more than twenty buildings. Our suggestion was for a compact and flexible center of just five buildings that would provide necessary centralization. This was the kind of university campus that Darcy Ribeiro had wanted.

I designed the university in Algiers, and the city's civic center, too, but work on the latter was halted soon after the excavation and grading had begun. Dejelloul had stepped down from office, so my designs for the center and the great monument that Boumedienne had commissioned were never built.

My relations with the French Communist Party were—and still are—marked by understanding and friendship. Marchais, Leroy, Gosnat, and Tricot,[97] for example, invariably treated me with warm consideration and appreciation. This kind of relationship allowed me total freedom to design the new party headquarters on Place du Colonel Fabien in Paris with the assistance of Jean Prouvé, Jean de Roche, and Paul Chemetov.[98] Our work was highly praised and today the building stands among the city's popular landmarks.

I remember the day President Georges Pompidou held a luncheon for all the architects on the jury of the Pompidou Center competition. The moment someone at the table made a favorable remark about the new PCF headquarters, Pompidou, never one to disguise his rightist politics, was obliged to agree, "Yes, it was the only good thing those Commies have ever done." The tribute was appropriate: everyone admired the building.

But it was not just the popularity of that building that tied me to those good comrades of the French Communist Party. Our shared views and political struggle were far more important than architecture. And we became good friends. How often Gosnat and his comrades took me to Parisian restaurants! Gosnat would lead the group and choose the menu, the wine, and the liqueur. What a wonderful friend he was! It was thanks to him and his confidence in me that the party headquarters was so well designed.

But fate has no favorites. One day, back in Rio, I received a telegram from him: "*Oscar, Marie est morte. Un immense malheur.*"[99] Both had been loyal and long-standing party members and they had been very close to each other. Gosnat could not bear the loss of his companion in life and in struggle, and he died shortly afterward. What a great pity! I remembered how he had asked me to join him on a long train journey from the Soviet Union through the Urals to China. I can remember the day of his funeral and the packed square; I was seated on the special dais as the party rendered its final public tribute to our unforgettable comrade.

While on the subject of friends from abroad, I must again mention those who worked alongside me in Brasília as we witnessed the birth and infancy of that splendid new capital so beautifully designed by Lúcio Costa. Now I seem to be watching flashbacks of my old companions from Brasília. We are all up to our knees in mud, or covered in the red earth and dust of those heroic times in the brush-lands. At the temporary hut where we worked, among other friends there was Nauro,[100] Sabino Barroso, Glauco Campelo, Montenegro, Pereira Lopes, Bulhões, Paulão. . . Even old Pará, our "jack-of-all-trades" at Novacap, who stood out because of his trumpeting voice.

I can see them all now, hunched over their drawing boards, totally absorbed by their work, caught up in our great crusade to build Brasília, come what may. At the end of the day, I see them riding buses back to their working-class homes. Some gathered in groups to comment on the day's problems and listen to wistful sambas amid high-spirited laughter. Others went to Cidade Livre (Free City) to dance at nightclubs and ogle the girls. The barren countryside naturally provoked a need for escape, although some individuals chose to remain alone with their thoughts. But bright and early next morning they were all there, ready for the bus ride back to our humble office, happy once again to immerse themselves in architecture.

I shared their enthusiasm and their worries, and the joy of seeing Brasília rising up from the middle of nowhere.

After some time the CEPLAN [planning center] office was closed down, so I hired architects residing in Brasília for specific jobs. There was Marçal, Cydno, and Birunga, and, later, João Filgueiras de Lima, a highly talented architect who has earned my unstinting praise for his splendid works throughout Brazil.

I recall a couple of things with particular satisfaction. One is my lifelong disdain for money; another is my urge to help people, to share with them and be useful to them.

Because I have had so much work, people obviously think I am a rich man. How do I deny this fact, given that so many of my buildings have made the headlines? How do I account for my travels and my projects in the Old World? Of course there were good times–but there were hard times, too. There were times of plenty and times of need. The good times were mainly when I returned from Europe, back in the 1970s. But that was all over so quickly that it took even me by surprise. No one knows just how many times I have worked for free, and how I have spent long months working without any payments coming in; or how I often invite friends along to share in the work. I have never been much concerned with money. In fact, I have always managed to put up with the uncertainties and unexpected turns in life.

What great satisfaction I took in buying an apartment for Luís Carlos Prestes! I remember that at the time my bank account was running low and I told his secretary, Acácio, to speed up the legal process. "Get that property deed through quickly, before I run out of cash!" This was an instinctive gesture of pure friendship. I so admired old Prestes; he was my friend and that was all that mattered to me. I have rarely felt so good about myself as I did that day.

April 1984. I was sitting out on boulevard Raspail, fondly watching the first leaves of spring appearing on the trees, people leaving their coats at home and cheerfully strolling along the boulevard under a blue sky. Something in the mild air positively dared one to go out for a walk, so I did. I used to roam the old streets of that Parisian neighborhood with their sober and regular buildings, their wrought-iron balconies and tall windows. I thought of the numerous celebrated writers, painters, and poets who had lived there so many years before and experienced those same joys and sorrows. I hardly ever bought anything. As in my first years as an architect, I was forced to live on a tight budget. I often window-shopped and then stopped at the newsstand to buy *Le Monde* and *L'Humanité.* Now and then I went into a bookstore to browse, leaf through a few books, maybe bump into a friend from Brazil and catch up on news from our distant and desolate homeland. Or I chatted with old Oscar Nitzke, a neighbor, who would spot me from afar. He invariably waved and smiled, eager to discuss New York, Wallace Harrison, and Le Corbusier with me. I used to sit alone over a demitasse of espresso for hours on end at La Coupole, serenely watching the passing of time–the same time which in my youth had seemed an everlasting promenade yet had now become so short. . . and so hostile. I sat at La Coupole and watched people going by, my mind preoccupied with yet another round of pressing financial problems. My friends warned me to hold down expenditures, to no avail. They said I wasn't getting any younger, etc., but I never paid any attention to them. I remember the day I stated in an interview, "I would be ashamed to be rich!"

I spent all I earned but I also helped many people, so the inevitable setbacks left me quite unperturbed. Unfortunately, in the course of this financial seesaw from abundance to shortage and back again, I took on too many commitments. Now I often think I could have dodged many of my troubles if I had heeded those warnings from my friends. But these doubts never haunt me for too long. They are always quickly vanquished by the certainty that I was quick to help friends in need–as if my money were theirs, too. I can live without this pointless self-criticism.

I am happy to say that I have always managed to put my financial problems behind me, starting with Pampulha, when I did the design for next to nothing in order to facilitate things for JK [Juscelino Kubitschek]. In fact, I drafted the whole complex for less than Candido Portinari charged him for a painting. Then came Brasília, and I did all the splendid buildings for the new capital on the miserly salary of a civil servant. I remember JK telling me on the telephone, "Oscar, you've got money problems. I want you to design the Bank of Brazil and the Development Bank. See that you charge the proper fee as established by the Institute of Architects of Brazil." My response was, "I can't do that. I am a civil servant with Novacap, a public employee."

. . . I finished my coffee at La Coupole. It was a beautiful spring day, the women seemed younger and less inhibited, the boulevard was packed with people, lively sounds, and merriment.

I got to live in two apartments during my sojourns in Paris, the first on rue François Premier, the other on boulevard Raspail. I liked that neighborhood–it was authentic, and far from the tourists along the Champs Elysées.

Everybody enjoys strolling around Paris. If you are a curious person, if you have ever been moved by the history of France, Paris is even more interesting, a city where past and present merge to their mutual advantage. Besides the scenic attractions, there are museums, exhibitions, and art shows–the pleasures and entertainment that only such a well-established civilization and culture can offer.

We are in the late 1980s now, and I am walking down boulevard Raspail on my way to the Metro station. How many tales this place could tell! There is that little café where Sartre and Simone de Beauvoir had coffee and croissants every morning. Close by are the Dôme, Le Select, La Rotonde, and La Coupole, the favorite restaurants of the spirited and enlightened bohemians of 1930s Paris. All this belongs to the past. Life has become harsher and more difficult. The informal, rebellious groups of the past are now dissolved, victims of the call "not to be involved" which Konrad Lorenz[101] points out in his analysis of the drama of life in the metropolis. Nevertheless, in France and particularly in Montparnasse, there is still a certain uniqueness that is hardly found anywhere else: the festive but popular and elegant atmosphere of La Coupole, the small

streets off the boulevard where great artists such as Modigliani used to live, and this nonchalant way of life, this savoir faire, that sometimes reminds me of our friends in Copacabana. This explains, for example, how a tailor who specialized in garment alterations was found waiting for his few customers at a nearby bar, chatting with friends; or the romantic figure of the Spanish guitarist, always wearing a hat, playing his instrument all day long without ordering anything. He seemed happy just to nurture the bohemian image he built up for himself and which suited him well.

On my way to the Metro I take in everything: storefronts, passersby, the day awakening in Montparnasse. A cool breeze shakes the leaves of the old chestnut trees greening in anticipation of summer. The boulevard is so lovely! I reach Vavin, feed my card through the ticket turnstile, and take the first train. I find a seat and then look around with interest at the other passengers. There are so many people of color in Paris! It disturbs me to think of our brothers in Brazil, who are so much poorer and far more aggravated by life.

There is a chubby, healthy-looking young woman sitting in front of me—she must be a country girl—with her bag secure between her knees. She glances at her fellow passengers and the passing scenery, but her thoughts are surely of far-off places. Studying her face, I try to imagine the various problems she might have in life. Alternately apprehensive and calm, she lets escape an uncontrollable smile of satisfaction. We really do find the same things everywhere we go in this world. The same contradictions, the same joys, and the same sorrows!

Beside me is a friendly old man, tieless like myself. He is busily examining his city: the usual seven-story buildings of the residential areas of Paris, their neat windows and blinds and small, flower-covered balconies suggesting a civilized and joyful people. Now and then a park appears out the window. These are cozy little tree-lined squares with children playing, young people courting, and old people perched on benches, dreamily watching life go by. Now we are nearing Passy, halfway to my destination. The train emerges on the surface track so we face the bridges and barges on the Seine, full of light reflecting in the water like a Monet.

The chubby girl gets off and a youth sits beside the old man, and with a friendly slap on the knee, says, "*Et alors?*" "Well," replies the man, as if there was no other possible answer, "We're in the government with the socialists." And the young man continues: "What about the Americans?" The old man retorts: "The Americans!

They just gave Mitterrand the opportunity to show them that it is up to the people of France." François Mitterrand had just been elected president [and the United States had attempted a veto on Communists forming part of the government alliance].

I wanted to hear more of this interesting conversation, but the train was pulling into the Champs Elysées station and it was my turn to get off. Taking to the sidewalk with a heavy heart, I began thinking of my own country and how our people were so politically backward, and how the reactionaries must have hated hearing the news of the left's electoral victory in France. That was wonderful news, and the French people cheerfully celebrated it by dancing into the early hours at Place de la Bastille.

I entered my office building and pressed the elevator button. Piped background music kicked in—but not the "Internationale," of course.

Also in Paris, I went to see Vinícius de Moraes perform. He was very pleased to announce my presence from the stage: "The architect Oscar Niemeyer is here with us tonight." I sat there listening to him singing, very much at ease, wearing his sailor cap, glass in hand.

We met again the next day. He was off to Chile to see Ferreira Gullar, a dear friend and great poet. Instead of Brazil paying him the tribute he deserved, the dictatorship had forced him into exile.

I have traveled to many lands and met a great many people. I have been to Lebanon, Italy, Algeria, Egypt, and even Saudi Arabia. In Italy I saw Giorgio Mondadori[102] again; I had met him years before in Rio, and back then he had asked me to design a building for his Milan publishing house. He had seen the Itamaraty Palace (Ministry of Foreign Relations) in Brasília, with its columns, and wanted something similar for his own offices. So I went off to Milan to view the site.

I have met few people like Giorgio Mondadori: cheerful, dynamic, with a happy-go-lucky attitude toward the good things in life. He greeted us with such a kind, warmhearted manner that I felt as if we had known each other for years. I remember having lunch at his house. He took me out to the garden and there we were playing soccer with his kids, Lopes and I running around after the ball, trying to score, and Giorgio as goalkeeper!

It was in this fraternal spirit that we supervised work on his offices for several years. When it was finished the tall columns and distinctive spans lent it that touch of creativity that he been looking for. Like Mondadori, I had the Itamaraty columns in mind when I designed his headquarters, but the result was very different: it was sturdy and monumental, with inventive, varied spaces. This was the architectural freedom I had always sought. For the first time in my architecture career a colonnade had emerged in a very distinctive style.

Years later, Giorgio was set on building another office in downtown Milan and again he looked me up in Rio. I drafted a design for him, but zoning problems eventually blocked construction. I remember him writing to me, "I've given up hope of getting clearance for construction, but I'm going to send you thirty thousand dollars for the design work anyway." I refused to take the money. I explained that in flying to Rio he had proved his real interest in my work, and that was sufficient reward for me. But my good friend Giorgio persisted in his intention and said I could give the money to the Oscar Niemeyer Foundation. I still refused. If I had taken the money, his journey and my work would have lost that fraternal spirit that I found so satisfying. Cecília Scharlach,[105] who recently stopped off in Milan, told me she had met Giorgio and heard him say I was his favorite architect. It's good to know these things, and to recall how Giorgio and his aide, Calanca, were so considerate and helpful.

I made many good friendships in Italy, where I designed the FATA offices in Turin with the aid of architect Massimo Gennari, then joined his team in drafting a pilot study for a stadium in Italy. I worked with other Italians, too, such as Tozzini, Frederico Motterle, and Lionello Puppi.[104] I am indebted to the latter for the book he generously wrote on my architecture.

Italy is so beautiful, and our Italian brothers are such good people, so fun-loving! I greatly enjoyed touring Rome, Florence, and Venice. It was a delight to see such enchanting art; the works of Palladio, Brunelleschi, Filippo Calendario; and the Doges Palace.[105] And to feel a nation advancing happily on the road to freedom and socialism.

I remember one particular Sunday in Italy—one of those typical Italian Sundays that De Sica portrayed so well in his films. From the platform at the railroad station in Milan, I watched as my colleague Marcos Jaymovitch struggled to stow our luggage on the train. A crowd of people shouted and gesticulated as everybody attempted to store their baggage at the same time. It was so confusing, so discouraging, that I gestured to him from a distance to tell him I had changed my mind about taking that train. My friend was baffled, but he understood me; he set about retrieving the suitcases he had worked so hard to get on the train. We left the station and looked for a car rental office, pleased with our decision.

"We only rent cars for weekends," they told us. We exchanged unhappy glances, since we were well aware that our trip would take much longer. Even so, we agreed to the terms, since we had no alternative. We knew we would not harm anyone and that in the end, everything would turn out all right, which always happened, and this made us feel happier about the whole business. So we got into the rented Alfa Romeo and set off for the Straits of Gibraltar and Algeria. What a journey! We passed vineyards of fine Italian wineries, the quaint villages of white houses with old church belfries towering over the scene. Then came Sicily with its Mafia organizations, the Sacred Family, the spirit of solidarity that inspired people to challenge the prejudices of the bourgeoisie. I recalled the island's heroes, like Giuliano, who led the youthful fighters of his age from his hillside stronghold. One night, we slept in an old medieval hotel, sober and silent, whose enormous stone columns recalled that period of intransigence and austerity.

We crossed to Algeria and spent two months there before driving to Paris. When we handed in the rental contract we had signed with the Italian firm, the rental office attendant was astonished. He told us that the car had been considered stolen and the insurance company had paid for it, so the company had suffered no loss. And, with a smile of collusion, he suggested, "Just park the car over there, and we'll forget the whole thing." The fact that we had driven around Europe for months in a "stolen car" somehow added a touch of adventure to our trip that we can only now appreciate.

I was very fond of Algeria. The country's conquest of freedom had brought about a wonderful transformation that I could sense in the euphoria and easy laughter of its people, who had been so horribly oppressed and so dreadfully humiliated. This joy in victory was to be seen everywhere: in the packed cafés, the streets, the squares, and on the faces of our Algerian friends as they proudly showed us film footage of the hard-won victory.

The old Casbah was the center of the armed struggle; from there, courageous Algerian women had set out to smuggle arms through checkpoints manned by colonial armed forces and delivered the instruments of revolution to their menfolk on the other side.

On my second day in the country I met President Boumedienne and found the same enthusiasm in him, too. He was a "monumental" figure, as André Malraux remarked in his memoirs of Mao Tse-tung: tall, looking you straight in the eye, wearing a fine combat uniform.

My major project in Algeria was the University of Constantine campus. The leaders most closely involved in the development of the work were Boumedienne, Dejelloul, who was then secretary to the presidency, and Mohamed Seddik Benyahiá, the minister of culture.

Algeria. . . oh, how I enjoy recalling those good old times and the house I lived in, the beautiful gardens around it, the flowers so dearly tended. I used to stand at the door and contemplate their vivid colors, and I could smell their perfume as the old gardener tenderly placed them in small pots he later arranged inside the house. The property included a park with a tennis court and soccer field. I even remember how we once played a very enjoyable game of soccer there. Occasionally I strolled around the park, checking out the vegetation: the thick palm trees with their layered trunks, the caladiums and philodendrons that reminded me of my tropical homeland.

In the evenings friends dropped in to visit or phoned me to discuss work. There was the high-spirited talk of Jorge Vale[106]—a great companion—who kept us laughing with his playing around. There was Edgard Graef, Pereira Lopes, Jorge Moreira, Marçal, Cydno, Montenegro, Fernando Burmeister, and Fernando Andrade,[107] all ready and willing to go to battle for top-quality design work.

But everything changed when Boumedienne died. We left the country and anxiously waited for news of our projects. Was the work in Algiers going ahead? Were our designs being faithfully implemented? One day I read in the newspapers that Benyahiá had been seriously injured in a plane crash. At the Paris hospital where I went to visit him, I found the minister bedridden, weak, and very thin, but recuperating. I could tell that he was touched by my visit when, on leaving, he silently took my hand in a gesture of friendship. Time passed and we all had almost forgotten the accident when, on a return trip to Algeria, his plane crashed. Another friend, a noble intelligence, lost forever.

I remember Algiers with deep nostalgia: its packed cafés, the white row houses the French built near the port, the Casbah, and the tough Algerian people striving to preserve their cultural heritage. I perceived in my Algerian friends many of the traits of my Brazilian brothers, that same optimistic laughter. My companions—there were almost thirty of them—often went without the comforts they had become accustomed to in the past. Their apartments were shabby and inconveniently located, and this produced a sort of permanent depression in some of the more fragile among them. But the majority realized that the country had just been through a grueling war of liberation so many things were as yet disorganized.

Our colleague Arakawa[108] had the most uncomfortable lodgings but was nevertheless the most optimistic of them all. Out of concern for his situation, one day I asked, "How are things?" "Just fine," he answered smiling. "And the women?" I asked teasingly. He responded with two triumphant fingers in the air. "Two of them!" We laughed at his optimism. These issues were not easy to resolve in that attractive and generous country!

I felt removed from everything: family and friends, the mountains, the ocean and the beaches of my country. I just had to go home. One day, I don't know why, the distance suddenly seemed to become more heartrending. I wrote the following lines, which I stuck on the office wall:

I am far from everything
From everything I love,
From that beautiful land
Where I was born.
One day I'll throw it in,
I'll hit the road,
And be back in Brazil,
That's where I want to live.
Every man in his own place,
Each one in his own home,
Joking with his friends,
Watching the day go by.
I want to watch the stars,
I want to feel life,
And be back in Brazil,
That's where I want to live.
I'm up to here,
Can't get over this flu,
Sick of hearing nonsense
Can't help myself through.
One day I'll have had enough,
I'll throw the towel in,
And be back in Brazil,
That's where I want to live.
This place is no good to me,
It is good for nothing,
I've made up my mind,
Nobody will stop me now.
Screw the job,
And this world of shit,
I want to be back in Brazil,
That's where I want to live.

Every time I went back to Pampulha I was sad and disgusted to see things being altered in such poor taste. The casino was converted to a museum; the yacht club was expanded and a wall built around it that ostensibly blocked it from the view of park visitors; and the dance hall, which was once a lively meeting place, was eventually also converted to a museum. The yacht club, the facade of which matched the unique architectural style of its interior, was transformed into a huge restaurant that bears no resemblance to the original plan. An architect's task is anything but easy!

Years later–in 1985, if I am not mistaken–Tancredo Neves, then governor of the state of Minas Gerais, José Aparecido,[109] and I attended the ceremony where the Pampulha complex was granted official landmark status. It was said to have launched an innovative architectural style that eventually spread throughout the world. "It is the only independent branch of contemporary architecture," said architect Marc Emery, director of *L'Architecture d'aujourd'hui* in Paris. The preservation measures adopted for Pampulha were insufficient, however, and today the investment required to restore the complex is impossible to secure. As a result, Pampulha today is surrounded by mediocre buildings that disrupt the architectural purity of its original design.

Today I stopped by my daughter Anna Maria's art gallery. As I was waiting for her there, I fell to recalling past episodes of our family life. We used to get very agitated, Annita and I, every time our daughter came down with a fever. Of course, this was a normal thing that happened to all children, but as parents we always panicked and spent the whole night at her bedside!

In the years that followed we brought her up with loving care and saw her grow into a young girl. We became concerned with her future. Would she find someone who would understand her? Would she and her husband be mutually forgiving, capable of living in peace and harmony as a happy couple?

But marriage is always an unpredictable adventure, full of surprises, whose outcome only time can tell. Unfortunately, her marriage was not as successful as we had wished it to be. Anna Maria went through some difficult times after that, and we were forced to witness her predicament from a distance, unable to intervene.

She never gave up. As the intelligent and hardworking woman she is, our daughter has pulled through all the trials that life has sent her way. Now, here I am waiting for her in the art gallery she has founded and made famous thanks to her own competence and nothing else. Anna Maria plunged into work, day and night, in her attempt to overcome her greatest sufferings, such as the painful loss of her daughter Ana Cláudia in a terrible car crash. She still carries this immense and unforgettable sadness in her heart.

Occasionally we visit her at home in São Conrado. I admire the warmth with which she welcomes visitors! Despite her busy work at the gallery, Anna Maria still finds time to nurture her friendships. These are mostly with artists, younger people who drop by the gallery. She has always sought to motivate those in whom she spots talent and the will of achievement that are essential in the art world. And I am proud of our beloved daughter, her dauntless spirit, and her courage in view of the inevitable adversities that life, so often perverse, holds in store for us.

During automobile trips to Brasília, my greatest distraction was to observe cloud formations in the sky. What numerous and unexpected possibilities they suggested! Now they formed mysterious, towering cathedrals—most certainly, the cathedrals of Saint-Exupéry; now, ruthless warriors or Roman charioteers crossing the skies; now, outlandish monsters racing swiftly with the wind; and, more often (because I always looked out for them), lovely and vaporous women reclining on the clouds.

In no time, however, everything changed. Cathedrals dissipated into a white mist; warriors changed into unending carnival parades; monsters sought shelter in dark grottoes, only to ·reappear further down, even more frenzied; and women slowly frayed away, growing

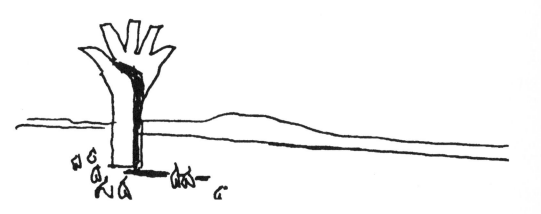

thinner and thinner until they were transformed into birds or black snakes. Those cloud figures looked so realistic that I often considered photographing them, but I never did.

Watching clouds remains my favorite pastime when I travel. I enjoy trying to decipher them, as if I were in search of an auspicious and long-awaited message. One day, however, the sight was even more breathtaking. I saw a beautiful woman, as rosy as a Renoir figure, with an oval face, full breasts, flat stomach, and long legs entwined with the white clouds in the sky. For a while I watched her, completely in awe, fearing that she might suddenly vanish. But those summer afternoon winds were on my side and for a long while she just floated there, gazing at me from a distance, as if inviting me up to play with her among the clouds.

Finally my fear was justified, and slowly my sweetheart vanished into thin air: her arms were elongated as they reached out in despair; her breasts soared as they detached from her body; her long legs coiled into a spiral, as if she did not wish to leave. Only her alarmed and sad eyes remained staring into mine, growing bigger. Then a large and heavy black cloud took her away from me. For a while I restlessly followed her with my eyes and watched as she struggled with the enfolding clouds and the raging winds that mercilessly tore her apart.

Just then I realized that the wicked metamorphosis I had been witnessing closely resembled our own destiny. After all, we are born, grow up, struggle, die, and then disappear forever, just like that beautiful woman in the clouds.

It is an ominous evening. A warm wind indicates a change in weather while flashes of lightning crisscross the heavy Copacabana skies, announcing an impending thunderstorm. I look up to a starless sky. Streets are empty, as if everyone senses, like me, that something is about to happen. The strong wind blasts against the glass panes of my apartment windows and I gaze apprehensively at the infinite cosmos. The gloomy sky and threatening atmosphere herald a gusty wind that howls around the street corners. Gradually at first, large raindrops dot the pavement, and soon a downpour falls heavily over the helpless city. In no time the street becomes flooded, leaving curb and sidewalk underwater. Cars pass by slowly, forming waves that deposit mud rings in apartment building entrances.

Fascinated by an enraged Mother Nature, I simply look on, remembering how very different everything used to be many years ago: Rio's population density, the number of vehicles on the streets, the effective sewer system, and fewer flood hazards. I remember how good it was to sleep peacefully, lulled by the gentle noise of raindrops falling on rooftops. I would lay there imagining the fields and forests happily welcoming the blessed rain; the flowers growing much prettier in the humid and bountiful soil. Even the waterfalls praised the rain graciously with their invigorated songs, and the sea became calmer, appeased by the arrival of rain, its ancient and sweet companion.

Nothing like that is happening now, when I think sorrowfully that soon the city will be inundated; that the noise of raindrops will be muffled by the thick slabs of penthouse roofs; that the homes of our poor compatriots will be washed out by the flood, and that these people will be left helpless, homeless, and hopeless in this loveless environment in which we all live. The morning newspapers will bring the calamitous headlines. Distressed city officials will once again pledge their unrestricted support to the victims, while shanty-town dwellers seek to rescue from the debris whatever is left of their shacks. In their gated fortresses, the bourgeoisie will be wondering whether the beaches have been raked clean for their daily jog. And time will pass uneventfully until a new flood takes over this helpless

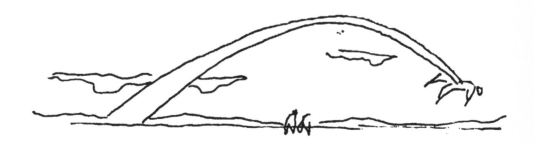

city. Then, other shanties will be destroyed, as if nature concurred with the hideous discrimination that so burdens the world.

On one occasion, I was dining with friends at Nino's restaurant in Copacabana when two younger couples walked in. One of the men immediately began to shout out against "brown-skinned socialism" and Communists. He did so in such a peevish manner that I thought his remarks must be directed at me. What could I do? I was eighty years old; he was half my age and six feet tall. This was probably exactly what made me react. I payed the bill and left the table as if headed for the door, but then I came back alone and hit him. People rushed to separate us. I had been punched in retaliation, and blood ran down my face.

The next day, without asking me, my cousin Carlos Niemeyer burst into the man's office. Frightened, the aggressor threatened to request police protection. Darcy Ribeiro was angry over the incident, and Brizola called me that night with sympathetic words. I refused to dwell on the matter. In fact, my name had not been mentioned and I felt rather guilty for having started a fight. I did not really understand why I had acted so impulsively. A few days later, I was talking about the incident with my friend João Saldanha in my office. He advised me, "If you draw your gun, aim low, because the recoil brings up the gun barrel."

National Congress complex, Brasília, 1958-60

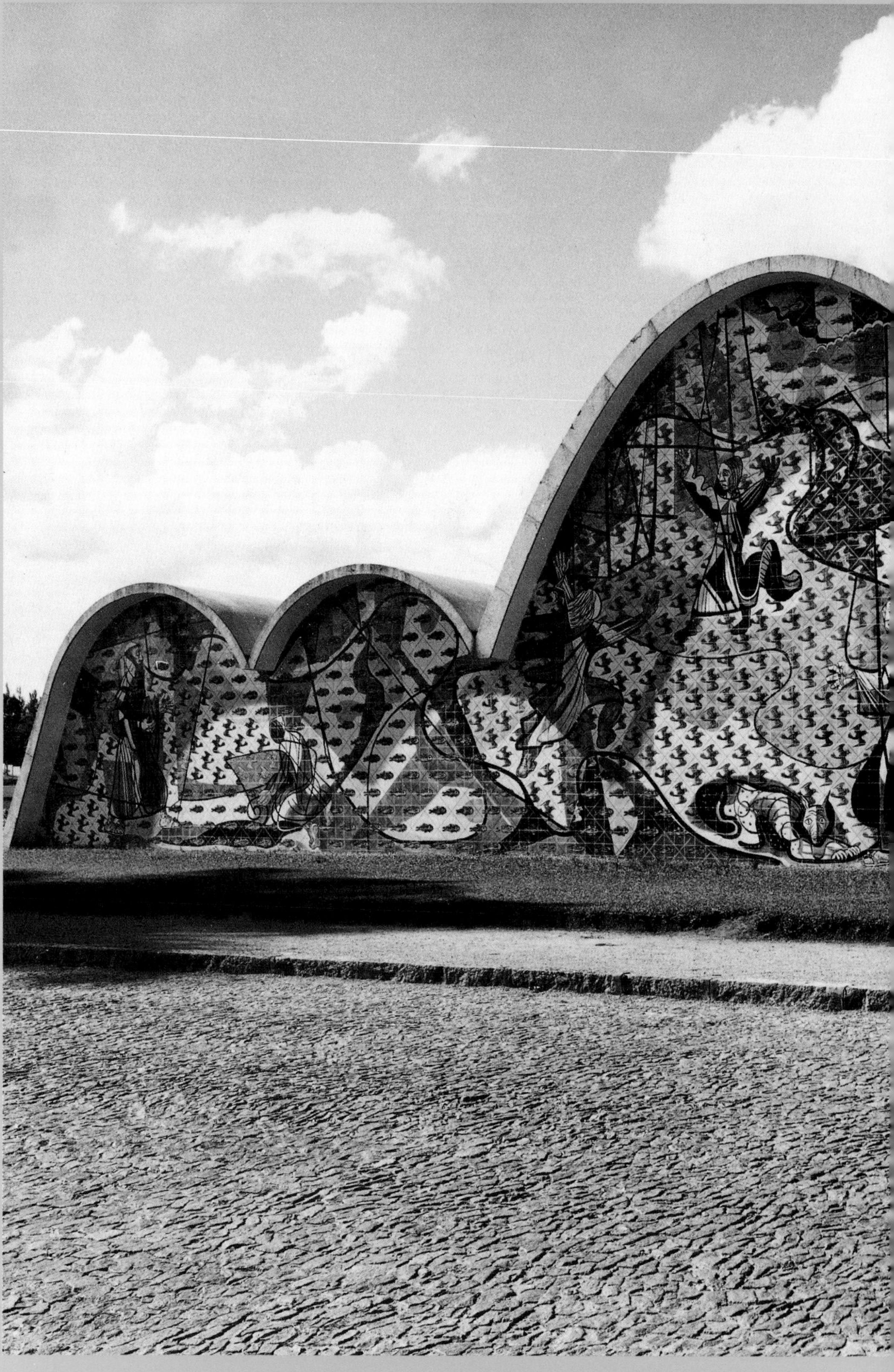

Chapel of São Francisco de Assis, Pampulha, 1943-44

Niemeyer (center) with Israel Pinheiro, selecting the site for the Alvorada Palace, Brasília, 1957

Niemeyer (right) with José Aparecido, 1980s

Ribeiro de Almeida, my grandfather, began his legal career as a judge in Maricá, his hometown. A street was later named after him, as other streets had been named after our cousin, Macedo Soares.

I myself have never been to Maricá. All I know of the city is what my grandmother told us, that she used to send her servant to buy shrimp in Ponta Negra. And there was also Galdino Duprat, the genealogist, who insisted that I was related to the Indian chief Araribóia,[110] whose son, so he said, had married an Almeida girl, supposedly a family relation.

I knew that Horácio de Carvalho owned a farm in the area, with the type of old colonial farmhouse that I had always wanted but certainly would never be able to afford. So Horácio's telephone call to me one day came as a delightful surprise. "Oscar, I've split up the farmland I own up there and the house is now yours. You're the only person capable of restoring it," he said. Such a brotherly attitude caught me off-guard, so it was only the next time I spoke to him that I managed to thank him properly.

I went to see the place, and there it was, my favorite colonial farmhouse with a sprawling roof, tall and identical windows painted blue, and a wide veranda that was an extension of the living room, in the Portuguese style. There was also a small chapel with a cross and conventional stained-glass windows built in a prominent location on the property, as dictated by the religious conviction of the colonial era. Close to the house was the old brick terrace used for drying coffee beans, the forested hillside, and a creek flowing in the rocky terrain. Further in the distance was a most beautiful man-made reservoir.

The next time I spoke to Horácio, another surprise was in store for me. "Listen, Oscar, Lily wants you to have the lake, too. She says the house is no fun without it."[111]

I thought of the memorable old times and the long-lasting friendship behind all this, a bond that developed silently but constantly despite the absences our diverse lives occasioned. My mind went back in time to our jaunts around the Lapa neighborhood and the cabarets. That was the old Rio, still unpolluted and undominated by vehicles, caressing our young spirits in the silent, wee hours of the morning. Later in our lives we had gone our separate ways. Horácio became editor of the *Diário Carioca* and with his charm and ability had become influential in the country's political scene, while I remained absorbed in my architecture. Every time we met, however, the conversation immediately turned to Café Lamas and our old and dear companions. We fondly recalled those events from the past, the inconsequential, everyday incidents that had marked our close friendship. The Café Lamas, the pool tables, the old Lapa district that Di Cavalcanti so enjoyed, our group of friends strolling arm in arm, too young to feel the weight of life in a world that seemingly had paused momentarily to let us live it up a bit.

Now freshly whitewashed, the farmhouse suddenly resembles an antique drawing by Debret.[112] Trees that have grown old with the house over the centuries seem to protect it with their leafy branches. The chapel dominates the property, whereas the farmhouse with its white and simple architecture humbly takes refuge here.

I am rereading this passage slowly, pondering my words carefully. I want to sound dignified and natural in light of this friendship. Finally, I wonder if I should even publish this account of a moment in time that recalls affection and solidarity, an episode that touches and concerns me alone.

I have just finished designing the Memorial da América Latina complex at Israel Pinheiro's request. A wistful feeling comes over me as I look at an old picture of Brasília. The site is still deserted, no houses yet, no trees, no flowers. There they are, old Israel Pinheiro, Moacir de Souza, Peri France,[113] myself, and other colleagues. We had gone to choose the site for the presidential building, the Alvorada Palace. The photo shows our enthusiastic group standing up to our knees in the underbrush, anxious to start work on the building and the nation's new capital. Israel was the leader of the group, with his assertive and optimistic personality. The backlands all around us are bare, hostile, and silent. We are far away from everywhere, at the end of the world.

Israel was a wonderful person, a paragon of hard work and determination who inspired us daily back in those first years of Brasília. Dawn had hardly broken when he would be out running around the sites, tending to any urgent changes or orders, looking after transportation and lodging. Eschewing bureaucracy, he took it upon himself to arrange every necessity, and his congenial and communicative presence was a great encouragement to us.

Of course we had our arguments, as is inevitable with a project of that nature. All our arguments were about the project schedule. Israel, for good reasons, fought to maintain his deadlines while I, the designer, claimed priority for my architecture.

We became such good friends that after Brasília was built, when Israel became governor of the state of Minas Gerais, he asked me to design the main government building there. I did the work for nothing and wrote to him that he should designate the money thus saved for the renovation of the hotel in Ouro Preto. My good friend Israel was so moved that he framed the letter, which to this day is still hanging on the wall of the governor's building in Belo Horizonte.

I gaze at the photo again. What a metamorphosis! The landscape was entirely transformed as Brasília bloomed like a flower in the middle of a desert, rising up within the spaces and scales created by its urban planner, dressed in the whimsical fashion of my architecture. The brushland of old was now covered with buildings and people, bustle and noise, joy and sorrow.

Thus Man intervenes in Nature, turning it into the theater of his illusions. The main performer in this act of magic, which so moved my Brazilian compatriots, was Israel Pinheiro, Juscelino Kubitschek's closest and most effective associate.

Galdino Duprat da Costa Lima was an intelligent man who claimed noble ancestry, so we would tease him until he responded with crude insults to everyone's mother. But he was a rather unusual nobleman. In 1945, when I joined the PCB, Duprat decided to follow me, arguing that he would be fighting the bourgeoisie. He was hot-tempered and overly proud, and we thoroughly enjoyed seeing him provoked, furiously threatening us all. But we also loved his company; he was amusing, a good friend, a great personality.

Since he was married and on a tight budget, any expense we forced him to incur, even a cup of coffee, made him complain angrily and remind us that he had a wife and child to keep, that he was a man with responsibilities. I recall the day some ten or fifteen of us were having lunch in a restaurant in Leme, and we agreed that the person holding the banknote with the lowest series number would pay for the whole gang. Duprat, of course, refused to take part. Finally, when the loser told the waiter, "I'm paying for everybody, except for that gentleman over there," Duprat sensed he was the butt of the joke. He stood up, roundly cursed us all to hell, and stormed out the door.

On another occasion, we were playing cards at the Clube dos Marimbás when Duprat left to go to the bathroom. We took advantage of his absence to deal him a spectacular royal flush. On his return, he was overjoyed to see his hand, but somebody called off the game with the excuse that there were too many cards in the pack. Duprat cursed us all furiously and stormed out. Feeling a bit remorseful, we set out to look for him unsuccessfully around the neighborhood. But these little squabbles never really amounted to anything. In fact, he enjoyed them, and we would joke about them the following day.

When Duprat was accused of being a Communist and was fired from his post at the Port Engineers' office, I looked up Rodrigo M. F. de Andrade to try to get Duprat a job at SPHAN. A few months later, Rodrigo, who hardly knew Duprat and was unaware of his love of authority, assigned him to head SPHAN in Recife, whose director had taken a leave of absence. Duprat's first move at SPHAN was to send Rodrigo an official letter demanding the dismissal of writer Gilberto Freyre,[114] who was a long-standing employee there but never showed up for work. Gilberto's distinction and renown were of little concern to him.

Duprat was no coward—on the contrary, he would start an uproar against any act of aggression. What is more, the day a nephew of his was assigned as an aide to the Navy minister, Duprat suddenly felt much more important. One day we were stalled in traffic and a police officer was taking his time to wave us through. Duprat made moves to get out of the car and bellowed in an authoritarian voice, "I'm going to arrest this guy!"

I remember how we were once at the headquarters of the political police and an official refused to return Duprat's passport. Duprat angrily demanded the official's details: "What's your name? I think I'll fix you up with some unpaid leave." The police official was astonished by such audacity and said to the guard, "Take this man out of here before I arrest him."

Duprat was not well-off, and every time he heard us talking about our travels in Europe I felt he wished he could travel there, too. So I took him along with me on two or three trips. Even there, in faraway Paris, we continued with the same pranks and jokes. He once told me that he wanted to see the changing of the guard at Buckingham Palace, so I sent him there. Duprat went off to London and afterward told us enthusiastically of the great pomp of the parade, and how one day he had been jostled in line and felt so frustrated because he could not curse everybody to hell on account of his poor English.

One morning, I went with Duprat and an Algerian who understood Portuguese to get a view of Algiers from a scenic lookout above the city. On seeing the magnificent view of the Casbah spread over the Mediterranean, he could not help bursting out, "My French ancestors bombed the shit out of this place ages ago!" The Algerian, who knew all about Duprat's tall tales, responded with a smile.

Then there was the time we were in my office in Paris. Duprat had written a letter to a mayor in southern France inquiring about his possible family connection with the French monarchy. Since the reply had not yet arrived, we decided to play a practical joke on our friend. We had a letter typed in which the mayor declared that he could not locate the information requested because the Communists had destroyed the town's archives. Duprat picked up the envelope and sat down at a drawing board to read it at his leisure. From the other side of the office we watched for his reaction, as if a bomb was about to explode. And it did. After about fifteen minutes of silence Duprat began cursing everybody as if the world had come to an end. Unfamiliar with Duprat's eccentricities, our French colleague recoiled. He could hardly imagine that five minutes later we would be off together, arm-in-arm, to the Champs Elysées, laughing happily as if nothing had happened.

Sometimes we improvised little practical jokes that lasted five minutes or less. On one occasion I was driving into the city with Duprat, who was in the passenger seat completely wrapped up in his own thoughts. So I drove into a familiar gas station and positioned the car on the hydraulic platform. I then got out, leaving Duprat in the car, still daydreaming, and waved the attendant to raise up the lift. Suddenly finding himself all alone in midair, Duprat let loose every kind of curse he could think of. I burst into laughter and went for a coffee, and when he had calmed down again we got on with the journey.

After some time, I discovered a trick that effectively stopped his outbursts. At the height of a major row, I would say in a quiet and earnest tone, "Duprat, did you hear what happened at SPHAN?" And he would forget everything, anxious to hear the story I was about to invent. Ah, good old Duprat, what dear friends we were! And how we laughed at our pranks!

Centro Brasil Democratico (CEBRADE) was originally an idea that belonged to my friend Renato Guimarães, who discussed it with Luís Carlos Prestes in Paris and with the party Central Committee. The idea was, as he put it, to found the Brazil Democratic Center, a national organization with a presence in all the main states and with centralized direction that would allow it to be led with the appropriate blend of caution and vigor. As Renato saw it, it would be a nonpartisan organization in which Communists and other political forces who fought against the dictatorship could remain clandestine, yet open to the broadest possible participation in democratic sectors. CEBRADE would be a means of broadening political debate and opening up new forms of legal political action in society, thus helping to unify democratic, patriotic currents and speed up the process of change to a new regime.

Renato launched CEBRADE in Rio in the late 1970s, and at his invitation I began attending its meetings, initially held in my office and later in a rented apartment in a nearby building. CEBRADE was a very active organization that gathered together a large number of artists and intellectuals. Its members were so numerous that I could not possibly mention them all in one book; however, it was interesting to see how the political struggle divides people in this world in which power and ambition are almighty.

After its initial phase, CEBRADE began to organize concerts of Brazilian pop music to raise funds for conferences, study courses, and other activities on its program. One concert held at Riocentro mall, in Jacarepaguá [a southern Rio de Janeiro district], ended up having great impact and influence on the country's political life. On the evening of the performance, two army officers attempted to set off bombs at the concert venue, which was packed with more than twenty thousand people. They were killed when the bombs blew up in their own car in the parking lot. To date this vile deed is remembered as a symbol of the violence of the black years of dictatorship. It proved that CEBRADE really was a thorn in the government's side, and that this regrettable episode was an important factor in hastening the fall of the military regime. As democracy returned, CEBRADE left the scene, but it was a major movement of fellowship and solidarity that could still be revived if, as Renato said, the defense of liberty and democracy should call for its comeback.

As I read over these pages, I feel that I should add something about my friend Luís Carlos Prestes, one of the most principled individuals of our times, a man who has won respect even from sworn enemies. He is so genuine, so true and honorable that he stands out like a beacon in this world in which falseness and collusion are all too common.

His story is well known to all of us. He dared to organize the protests throughout Brazil, from north to south, at the head of his heroic column.[115] There was his adherence to Communism; his nine-year imprisonment, isolated from the outside world; his pregnant wife killed in a Nazi concentration camp; his release; and his vigorous stance in the face of adverse political conditions. Then came Hitler's defeat, the party's official recognition, and Prestes's acclamation in the great rallies of 1945 and 1946. He was the "Knight of Hope" that the Brazilian people were waiting for. But the period of euphoria was short-lived. In 1946, the Communist Party was declared illegal again and Prestes went into hiding, only to return many years later with the same enthusiasm and fighting spirit of his youth.

It is now 1987 and Luís Carlos Prestes is eighty-nine years old. He is no longer a member of the PCB, but his struggle against social injustice continues to be a strong factor in his life as he lectures, radical, alone, and unbending, at universities, union meetings, factories, and political centers throughout Brazil.

Prestes often comes over to my Copacabana office. Surrounded by colleagues, he discusses Brazilian politics with the passion and lucidity of a young guerrilla. Everyone admires him. We are invariably moved by his unwavering revolutionary conviction. When he leaves, I take him to his car—a habit I picked up when he was under police surveillance and I was concerned for his safety.

In August 1987, at the insistence of some PCB comrades, I attended a meeting of the party leadership at the Brazilian Press Association (ABI). The room was packed, and most of the people I did not recognize. I suddenly realized that time had passed without my noticing it. Where were the old comrades I used to meet on these occasions, gathering together as if we were an inseparable family?

Salomão Malina, the new PCB secretary, chaired the meeting; beside him was Geraldão dos Santos,[116] who was actually running the affair. I was summoned to serve on the panel, as were others after me, and then the meeting began.

While all this was going on, I thought of the past. In 1945 our huge rallies filled the streets and entire stadiums. But only shortly after that came the return to clandestine meetings, threats against our party, and our unflinching determination. Now there was an atmosphere of tranquility that we had never known back in the hard times of repression and illegality. The meeting went on. From time to time, one of the most enthusiastic party members would shout out a slogan for all to chant. Everybody stood up and joined in with their fists raised and clenched to symbolize struggle. But I felt too embarrassed to join them, since this was in gaping contradiction to the conciliatory line that the party had adopted.

I was included among the alternates for the Central Committee, and when my name was read out, everybody stood up and applauded. Geraldão and Malina embraced me affectionately. I left the meeting with Nélson Werneck,[117] reminiscing about the old times in the party and the spirit of struggle and optimism that we had found so highly attractive.

Brazil. . . often I feel something of a Jacobin when defending my country abroad. I always refute criticisms, although they are often quite fair and meant as friendly advice. For some reason, however, I can never tolerate these criticisms. I remember feeling so angry in Paris one day when someone began to bad-mouth Brazil, its huge spending programs, its gigantic construction projects. What the country needed, they said, was a more realistic and thrifty policy. I could not help myself, replying that this was all quite natural, a kind of childhood disease, inevitable in developing countries. And I explained that Brazil was really a continent. A young country that justified everything. A force of nature.

If the talk drifted toward culture, I would burst out, "It is so very easy for us Brazilians to take over the world of imagination and fantasy! Our past is a humble one and every option is open to us." I would continue, "It must be so difficult for you people here to innovate, after spending your whole life around monuments!" And I would repeat my favorite motto: "We have a different task: to create today the past of tomorrow." But my audience usually consisted of friends, so the talk would move on to some other issue and there would be more fraternization as we discussed the troubles of the world.

Yesterday I read a book by Pablo Neruda that made me feel more at ease with my own nationalist inclinations and emotional outbursts. He writes of Chile, his "beloved Chile," of Parral, his "lovely home town." Just reading that line did me good! Like him, I love my country, with all its grandeur and its poverty; I love Rio, its beaches and mountains, its easygoing and uninhibited people. I really love this immense country of ours! From north to south, from the homeless and starving desperate northerners fleeing from the drought, to the shantytown dwellers on the hills of Rio de Janeiro and their refusal to buckle under. I attempt to defend them when they are persecuted and surrounded by the implacable injustice of Man.

Dear reader, when shall we transform Brazil into a land of fellowship and solidarity? Our laboring brothers are getting poorer all the time. What can be done? Angrily, I think of Che Guevara's words: "An unarmed people does not even exist."

For several months I worked for José Aparecido in Brasília.[118] He was extremely considerate, and his courtesy and friendship encouraged me to complete the tasks I had set out for myself. He is so enthusiastic, and his affection and concern for the city is so evident, that I try to help him as much as I can in architectural matters.

Aparecido is an intelligent and determined man, full of plans and ideas for tackling large-scale problems on down to minor auxiliary works for this city that has grown too fast. Sometimes I accompany him on his visits to the poorer districts in the outskirts of Brasília known as satellite-towns. In no time he is surrounded by residents eagerly demanding that old promises–century-old promises, in fact–be fulfilled. They have implored one governor after another for a solution. Humble as the promises may have been, they are crucial to those struggling for subsistence within the odious system of social discrimination that capitalism has created. These people do not even ask for a house to live in, but merely a tiny lot, a small piece of this enormous land–which belongs to them, too, and which means nothing in this immense country, a real continent.

I then realized how misguided architects are when we plan huge housing complexes for the low-income population: prefabricated, modulated, cheap solutions that technology has now made possible. The reality of Brazil, I realized, is that our people live in such abject poverty that our poorest brothers just want a small lot where they can build a miserable hut.

Sometimes these pleas for help come from older people. It is plea they have repeated for many years, since the days of their youth, when the world seemed a better place. José Aparecido is touched and notes all their requests; he is moved to indignation by the poverty. I begin to think how difficult it will be for him, such a generous man, not to be able to solve the urgent and undeniable problems of the poor.

Human problems are not the governor's only concern. He is aware of Brasília's importance to the country as a whole. Thousands of tourists expect to see this city that was built overnight in a remote and solitary desert and now bursts with people. Aparecido understands all this and wants to conclude work on the city's monumental axis, assuring its crucial architectural unity–a unity already lost in other sectors of the city through lack of talent and negligence on the part of government officials. He is passionate about the importance of architecture over time, the moving power of a work of art, and the eternal power of the beauty that ancient peoples sought in ecstasy, and that to date remains attractive no matter what its origin and aims.

I often felt an urge to make sculpture. "You are the sculptor of reinforced concrete," people used to tell me, and I trusted that some-day I would actually become one. As time passed, I used my spare time to make a few sketches. I fantasized about creating large sculptures for public squares. They would be abstract, light, floating in air. Perhaps they would be surrealistic works that prompted viewers, somewhat awestruck, to take a moment to think about and try to decipher them.

I accept everything that is beautiful and well done. I have always been capable of identifying a common denominator of beauty and talent in the paintings of Picasso and Matisse, for example. I have appreciated sculptures by Henry Moore and Barbara Hepworth. I admired the purity in Brancusi; the lovely women created by Charles Despiau and Aristide Maillol;[119] lean figures by Giacometti; the Hellenic and Egyptian sculptures; and the beauty and movement of the *Victory of Samothrace.*

One day I told my friend Honório Peçanha[120] about my desire to take up sculpture. He gave me a sack of clay, a square wood board, and a large nail, which was all I needed to get started. But I never managed to use them; I was paralyzed by self-criticism. Nonetheless, many years later I did not have the courage to turn down the invitation to design both the Juscelino Kubitschek Memorial and the monument Tortura Nunca Mais (Torture: Never Again) comm-issioned by the Brazilian human rights organization of the same name.

In the process of meeting their destiny, individuals feel fulfilled when their hopes and beliefs are realized. To date I have only made protest sculptures. The first one I ever designed was the JK Memorial, which consists of a tall shaft, the curved top of which simultaneously shelters and highlights the former president's statue sculpted by Honório Peçanha. My objective was to defy the dictator-ship and its reactionary supporters, forcing them to look at Kubitschek's statue every day–Kubitschek triumphantly smiling down at the city that Lúcio Costa had designed and he had built.

Early criticism of the memorial sprang from the more right-wing reactionaries who viewed the work as a Communist emblem in which JK's raised arm resembled a hammer and the prolongation of the curved shaft, the figure of a sickle. I could never have left JK's statue standing loose on a pedestal, lost against the immense sky of Brazil's new capital. The "sickle" provided an indispensable frame for my creation.

For several weeks JK's sculpted figure lay on the ground, awaiting a solution. One day my friend Adolpho Bloch called me from the office of Mayor Lamaison.[121] "Oscar, I'm here with Dona Sarah,[122] and we have found a solution to the problem: we could erect a brick wall in place of the 'sickle,'" Bloch told me. "If you do that, I am going to protest," I replied. Astounded, he retorted, "You can't protest, the mayor is our friend!" And I concluded, "Then I'll protest against the military." Adolpho Bloch hung up the phone, his solution stymied. A few days later, President Figueiredo[123] broke the deadlock when he authorized the statue to be installed according to my original design. Had I not reacted, JK's statue would now be standing against a brick wall, devoid of its intended lightness and prominence.

The second sculpture I designed, Tortura Nunca Mais, was meant to keep alive the memory of that long and gloomy twenty-year period when political prisoners were tortured in Brazil. I conceived the sculpture as a human figure pierced by evil forces represented by an eighty-two-foot-long curved spear. As I had anticipated, when this sculpture was published, it divided public opinion. While some people criticized it as unnecessary provocation, others found it too poignant. For many years the more cautious individuals were reluctant to have the monument built. Only recently Darcy Ribeiro announced his resolution to install it at the entrance to the Campos University campus.

My third sculpture was the large-scale hand with a streak of blood running down to its wrist that I designed to represent an exploited and oppressed Latin America. This twenty-three-foot-tall sculpture has been installed at the Memorial da América Latina complex in São Paulo.

The fourth sculpture I designed was a memorial commissioned by the Metalworkers Union in honor of three workers killed by the reactionaries. My creation was so nonconformist, however, that it was blown up on the day of its inauguration by right-wingers who reacted with violence and desperation. The violent explosion shattered the glass windows of neighboring buildings. Notwithstanding direct threats and letters of protest, I suggested that the monument be re-erected with its exposed fractures and the following phrase, which I wrote: "Nothing, not even the bomb that destroyed this monument, is capable of deterring those who struggle for justice and liberty." To this day the monument, which for the first three days was guarded by a group of metalworkers, is still standing.

I designed a fifth sculpture in memory of a similar event involving workers killed during a demonstration in the city of Ipatinga, in the state of Minas Gerais. My sixth sculpture was commissioned by the Senegalese government as a memorial to the thousands of Africans forcibly removed from the city of Gorée–where the work is going to be erected–and sold as slaves in Latin America. The memorial consists of a 264-foot-tall concrete slab on which I carved the figure of a slave, an individual abducted from his homeland in those days of unspeakable violence.

Earlier in this book I mentioned the "persona," an indistinguishable individual I believe we have within ourselves who oftentimes interferes in our relationships. I first became aware of my persona after reading Monod and Jacob. I then realized that human characteristics are passed down from parent to child and resist the influential reasoning of the social environment. I realized that these characteristics are combined, though often imperceptibly, with pre-programmed physical traits. Later I began to view the human being as a house that can always be renovated. Like a house, one can repair its roof, replace door and window frames, paint walls, and patch ceiling leaks. However, like a house, it will always be inadequate if it has been poorly designed in the first place.

This is why, my friend, I tend to excuse so many slip-ups, so much negative behavior, both my own and that of other people, including those I deal with on a daily basis. I am sure we are not entirely responsible for our good qualities and our inadequacies. Certainly the environment influences all of this, improving the individual's inner structure or making it worse. But many times this control apparatus imposed by life and society fails to function. That is when, all of a sudden, people expose their true personalities.

One day in Paris, I was discussing this subject with my biologist friend Luís Hildebrando. "I don't agree with you, but neither can I argue with you," he told me. His Marxist side had detected in my commentary a fatalism that had never existed before.

When Jânio Quadros asked me to work on the Tietê River project, I realized this was my great opportunity to give São Paulo a new leisure district. The river had been walled in by two freeways, so I thought about relocating one of the thoroughfares farther away from the riverbed to create a beachlike environment that the city lacked. It would be a wonderful contribution to the city.

I would have loved to have executed that project. I imagined São Paulo dwellers strolling along the banks of the Tietê and, like in Copacabana, pretty women in bikinis, children playing on the shore of a clean and refreshing river. . . . Unfortunately, an unbelievable lack of common sense kept the project from going through. I agree it was an ambitious idea, one that required a considerable expropriation of land along the river. Only someone as dynamic as Jânio Quadros could have implemented it.

I worked on several jobs in the city of São Paulo and gradually made many friends there. Cecília Scharlach, Maria Amélia Melo, Hélio Penteado, Hélio Pasta, Paulo Mendes da Rocha, Ubirajara Giglioli, Ruy Ohtake, Eduardo Corona, Ciro Pirondi,[124] and Fernando Lemos are, among many others, the people I like and greatly admire in São Paulo.

My life has not changed at all, but there are few of us left at the Copacabana office. Projects are developed very competently at the office run by my granddaughter, Ana Elisa, and Jair Valera.[125] I draft a few jobs myself with my nephew, João Niemeyer, who is preparing for his chosen profession, one at which he is evidently talented.

I chat indiscriminately with everyone at the office. The staff includes Brandão, Rodrigo [M. F. de Andrade] and Aurélio; Amaro, my friend and driver; his son Eduardo; and Maria das Graças, who cooks for us.

Outside Rio I rely on aid from colleagues. In São Paulo, Cecília Scharlach, Maria Amélia Melo, Hélio Penteado, Hélio Pasta. In Brasília, Fernando Andrade and Carlos Magalhães. I have worked for many years with Carlos; in addition to possessing crucial technical skills he maintains an unwavering political position in defense of this city–a quality that I greatly admire.

My grandson Carlos Eduardo is now part of the office, in charge of photography and exhibitions. He is an intelligent and creative young man, a joy to have around. My other grandson, Carlos Oscar, is tending his father's farmland. Regrettably, his work keeps him far away from us. I have never known a young man so upstanding and sensitive. My granddaughter Ana Lúcia heads the Oscar Niemeyer Foundation. She constantly impresses me with her competence, fully aware as she is that the job involves not only preserving my work, but also cooperating with younger architects and giving the more established Brazilian architects the support and publicity they deserve. Ana Elisa I have already mentioned, but I should like to add that she is one of the most generous people I have ever met.

The rest of the crew consists of the great-grandchildren and great-great-grandchildren on the way. . . .

When the idea to build the Memorial da América Latina in São Paulo came up and I was commissioned with its design, I immediately realized how important this undertaking was for me. This cultural center was to convey an appeal, a message of faith and solidarity for all Latin American people. It would invite them to come together, share experiences, and fight more effectively on behalf of this highly neglected and endangered continent.

The Memorial da América Latina was erected with a great deal of technical skill and imagination: a set of white buildings boasting 231- and 297-foot-long beams and elegantly rounded concrete slabs– a beautiful, monumental complex that perfectly suited the grand initiative conceived by São Paulo governor Orestes Quércia.

For many months I closely followed the construction work and was quite moved by it. Despite having completely devoted myself to the project design, I felt that something was missing, something that would allow me to take part in the political nature of the cultural center, which was more important to me than its architecture.

Thus, to represent Latin America, I designed a large, concrete, open-palmed hand, its fingers slightly bent to convey despair, and a trickle of blood running down to its wrist. To explain the spirit of my sculpture, I wrote, "Sweat, blood, and poverty have marked our disjointed and oppressed Latin America. Now it is crucial that we readjust this continent, unite it, and transform it into an untouchable monolith capable of insuring its independence and happiness."

Thus the 23-foot-tall hand was erected. It represented a critique and a forewarning rather than a provocation. It brings to mind a shadowed past and a future full of hope and doubt. Our hope turned into bloodshed and revolt in 1989 as the United States invaded the small, unprotected country of Panama. This sort of criminal act should have roused the protest of all other countries that claim to be democratic nations—of all people who advocate democratic rule and the principles of equal rights, opportunity, justice, and freedom. The U.S. justification for the invasion—the defense of a democratic regime—is certainly preposterous, given that the U.S. government overtly supported Latin American dictatorships during many years.

At such times we must react. We must protest. We must not accept this criminal intervention into the affairs of our exploited and offended Latin America. This large concrete hand, an expression of my anticipated protest, thus acquires another significance. It is no longer a simple sculpture, but a plea that all visitors to the Memorial da América Latina become aware of the drama experienced by our brothers throughout this continent. Although still poor and underdeveloped, Latin America is fully aware of its rights, sorrows, and hopes.

As construction work advanced, we were faced with the inevitable question of artworks for the memorial. My concern was that I should be the one to select them and that they should be installed in their intended locations. Realizing I had a difficult problem before me, I decided to voice my opinion in an article published in the *Folha de São Paulo* newspaper. Thankfully, this resolved the issue, and I received the governor's authorization to select the proposed artworks. Because the integration of art and architecture is still misinterpreted, I think it is worth transcribing an excerpt of that article wherein I define the architect's role as coordinator of a building's furnishings and of the selection of artworks:

> False modesty aside, I can shamelessly affirm my position as the [Brazilian] architect who has included the

largest number of artworks in architectural designs. Gustavo Capanema, former minister of education and health, adopted this ancient practice in the construction of the ministry building. An intelligent and cultivated man, our friend entrusted this task to the architects he hired. Following our advice, he purchased works by Portinari, Celso Antônio, Bruno Giorgi, and Lipchitz. At the time, the latter was the sculptor who worked in close association with Le Corbusier. There was no public bidding. What is more, no one assumed the narrow-minded attitude of restricting the selection to Rio de Janeiro artists. The issue at hand was to complete a work of architecture; it was up to the architects–and the architects only–to resolve it.

I have always followed Capanema's example. Whenever possible, I have invited artists to collaborate on my designs. I first adopted this procedure in the 1940s in the Pampulha project, for which I assigned Portinari, Ceschiatti, and Paulo Werneck, and proceeded with Di Cavalcanti, Marianne Peretti, Athos Bulcão, Firmino Saldanha, João Câmara,[126] Bruno Giorgi, Honório Peçanha, and many others. I never forgot them, even when I was working abroad. In the Old World their work is integrated into my architectural

designs as examples of Brazilian creativity and culture. I am content and proud to have adopted these criteria, particularly when I remember that I was the one who commissioned Portinari's *Tiradentes*, a masterpiece of Brazilian painting, for a school in Cataguases. I remember how difficult it was to realize my idea! First I had to talk my friend Peixoto into having a mural painted on the twenty-meter wall I had designed. Then I had to take Portinari to Cataguases, which meant long hours driving down the dirt country roads.

Now, with the construction of the cultural center, I am facing the same problem again. Once more I must provide the necessary explanations, as if I were talking to schoolchildren. Every time an architect designs a building and sees his work on the drawing board, he visualizes it in its final version. Assuming that he feels passionate about his job, he is driven by curiosity and the urge to go deeper and examine shapes and spaces, wondering where a panel, mural, sculpture, or simply a black-and-white design might fit. While on this imaginary journey, he may start looking into details. Should the mural be painted in lively colors to stand out from the work as a whole, or in neutral colors to enhance it visually? Should the sculpture be light and abstract or represent a

beautiful woman? Should the drawing be linear or free or figurative? Furthermore, if the external walls are of exposed concrete, should they contrast–the designer wonders–with severe stone walls or with simple white masonry?

This is the creative act, the highly sought-after integration of art and architecture. It is the only way to create in a logical way, with a view to the indispensable unity and beauty of the work.

Many are the factors that guide an architect in his or her selection of collaborators, even–why not admit it?–a desire to keep working with long-time colleagues, aides, and friends who have proved themselves so many times in the joys and sorrows of the job.

In the Memorial project design I adopted my standard guidelines and requested works to enrich the building complex. There are sculptures by Bruno Giorgi, Weissman, and Ceschiatti; stained glass by Marianne Peretti; bas-reliefs by Bonomi, Caribé, and Poty; paintings by Portinari, Scliar, Gruber, Vallandro, and Arruda; embroidery by Tomie Ohtake;[127] and tiles by Athos Bulcão.

The memorial finally became what I had envisaged, thanks to the help of Fernando Andrade, Maria Amélia, and primarily Cecília Scharlach, who defended my plan with the unyielding determination of a revolutionary.

Today is Carnival Monday and I have spent the day alone at the Carlton Hotel in Brasília. I read an interview with Alberto Moravia and a short book by Borges; I wrote a little, then watched the rain beat on the window pane and the heavy clouds gather over the city. A strange feeling of melancholy seemed to take hold of me. Only in the evening did I finally switch on the TV.

It was the carnival parade. The São Clemente Samba School paraded by; their motif was "The abandoned child in this world of illusion." As I listened to the lyrics, I thought of the miserable poverty that afflicts our country, the poorest children wandering the streets, sleeping on sidewalks, while a privileged few enjoy all that money can buy.

Sitting in front of the television, I was moved by the rhythmic, repetitive music and by the lyrics that made me simultaneously happy and sad. On the one hand, here was dire poverty; on the other hand, a call of protest was arising out of that festive carnival atmosphere in which social contradiction and celebration exist side by side.

There are some aspects of the carnival parades that I have never appreciated. For example, the dancing and singing remind me of outdated things, of the days of slavery that should be long forgotten. For a few days the poor descend from their hillside shanties to celebrate, and the bourgeoisie surround them with flattery and applause, only to forget about them the next morning. I thought about how nice it would be if, as during carnival, the poor were to confront them with songs of protest. Unfortunately, this does not happen very often. The samba schools have to meet their expenses, and that means compromise; the usual songs are vague and romantic, harmless fantasies that do nothing for the century-old struggle against social injustice.

I don't know why I turned off the sound to write these words. Later I called a friend who told me, surely with a smile, "Oscar, don't cry." Of course I was not crying, although–who knows–perhaps I was close to tears. It was not just the poverty that hurt me, but also this enormous injustice that we must eliminate.

I enjoy talking about Lúcio [Costa], this great Brazilian I first met in the 1930s and to whom I am greatly indebted. I must go back in time to tell you about the occasion when he generously allowed me to spend some time in the office he shared with Carlos Leão.

Those were difficult times for me as a student, with a wife and daughter to support and living on the rent from a house we owned in Rio. Even so, unlike some of my colleagues I was unwilling to work in just any office, pick up solutions to the practical problems of the profession, and get paid for it. Not me. I preferred to work for Lúcio Costa for no pay at all. Today, when I think back to that period, I feel that I was not just a mediocre student who parachuted into Lúcio's office by chance. No, I had a vocation for architecture and I wanted to be a good architect.

I learned much about the real issues of architecture, the importance of our old colonial architecture, the idealism that the occupation demands. I remember the old times: leaning over Lúcio's drafts, impressed by the beautiful houses he designed and the exquisite drawings he made to present them. I liked his civilized manner, his courteous attitude, quite unlike Carlos Leão, who was more outgoing and happily took me around the downtown bars. I was not much help, but I did know how to draw, so I tried to please them, and we became good friends.

I admired his enormous talent, so genuine, which allowed him to become an urban planner practically overnight, creating the fine and welcoming city that is our nation's capital. Lúcio was an introvert who had been hard hit by the somber shadows that fate casts on our wretched lives. As a widower he became more distant and hermetic, although attentive to everything around him and always ready to stick up for old companions.

I was very happy one day to be able to suggest to the then-governor of Brasilia, José Aparecido de Oliveira, that we should include an area named for Lúcio Costa in the Praça dos Três Poderes (Plaza of the Three Powers), and I designed it with the affection that my old friend deserved.

In the old days of the PCB, where I learned so many things, the inexorable question of death sometimes came up in our discussions. Soon one of the more passionate members would lay down the line: "The important thing is the preservation of the human species." Despite my great esteem for the comrades, I could not bring myself to accept this. I was sure that my grandchildren and great-grandchildren would have the same forebodings about death.

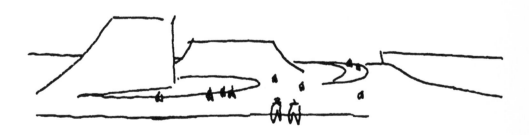

I was curious and I loved to read, particularly Sartre. I saw that there was a great deal of truth in his pessimism. It was no easy subject to raise. Some people had no interest in it; others, the more privileged, were unmoved and quite happy simply to enjoy the ephemeral pleasures of this world. Not even the state of destitution in which our poorer brothers lived was enough to move them.

Personally, I was convinced that truth cannot be slighted; one day it will triumph and be lasting and irrefutable. I realized that the universe was not made for us, and that, on the contrary, we were just a tiny part of nature. And I thought that the world could be a better place. Men could be conscious of their insignificance, could despise power and wealth, be brothers to the beasts of the earth and the fish of the seas. It would be an unbearable world to live in, my comrades promptly answered, without hopes, without fantasies, without the dreams that allow us to live better.

I would listen to them condescendingly. Yes, it is nice to dream, to forget unresolved problems and to fantasize, to give our imagination the free rein that leads us to conquer space and search among the stars for the answer to the enigma of this wonderful universe around us. As a veteran party member, I continued to say, Yes, we must dream, but we must do so hand in hand with our proletarian brothers.

I read these words and feel that as I age, a warm feeling of fellowship is taking over my heart, overcoming old resentments; I am seeing the good side in everybody, which does not, of course, erase my indignation toward the immense poverty throughout our world.

But joy and sorrow are our old and inseparable companions and, with a smile, I see that Communism has not died, as they have tried to tell us. My determination today is the same as always, the same unflinching determination with which Fidel, arm-in-arm with the Cuban people, confronts and shames the cholera of U.S. reactionary attitudes.

But life goes on, unjust and not at all too generous, so fragile and illusory that Sartre ends his book *Qu'est-ce que la littérature* with this ironic question: "*Est-ce que le monde serait meilleur sans les hommes?*"[128]

One morning I was entering the building where I work when a small boy approached to sell me some chocolates. He looked so weak, so sad and humiliated, that I gave him some money.

As I rode the elevator, his image took on another dimension; it was not only this abandoned child that concerned me, but the enormous poverty of which he was only a painful example. Few take it seriously, even when it becomes as generalized as it has in Africa, where starving crowds scramble for food supplies dropped from planes, as if more human contact were not needed to help them. Perhaps it is my age, but I could not help being so moved that I asked an assistant to bring the boy into the office.

We talked. I asked him where he was from. He said he was from Minas Gerais, from Caratinga. He had run away from home and was living on the streets, sleeping on the sidewalk near the viaduct in Lapa. He was eleven years old.

I asked him what he wanted to be. "A musician or a singer," he answered. I eyed him thoughtfully. How many poor boys like him had become men of great importance, in the most diverse professions! And I remembered Camus, Chagall, and our own Machado de Assis. How many talents are being lost in Brazil due to this permanent neglect of abandoned children!

I told him I would like to help him, but that nobody would keep him there against his will; he could leave whenever he wanted. I asked someone to take him out and get him some clothes–pants, shirts, and shoes. And when he came back washed and decently dressed, I began to appraise the scale of the problem. "The things you come up with!" my daughter Anna Maria said.

My cook at the office, Maria das Graças, offered to have the boy stay at her apartment. We agreed that he would be at the office during the day and she would take him home in the evening. So there was, provisionally at least, a place for him to live. But there were problems. He lacked the papers needed to enroll in school.

I talked to a friend. His wife kindly promised to look into the matter for me. Geraldão, my party comrade, suggested a school in the Mangueira neighborhood. For four days we lived through this disturbing saga. I felt that the boy was torn between going home or staying with his homeless peers, living and sleeping on the city streets.

He disappeared twice and turned up the next day, filthy and almost naked, wearing only his underpants. Everything else had been stolen from him. The first time, he seemed determined to stay away from home–"I'm going to stay in the Lapa." The second time, to our surprise, he preferred to go home.

With the little money I gave him, he bought a small camera and asked me to have a photo taken of the two of us together. After an entire day spent trying to obtain the police papers required for a minor to travel between states, the kid was off to Caratinga.

Of course, the fact that we were able to get him off the streets was a happy ending for us, but it matters so, so little compared to the incredible scale of abandonment that affects thousands of children in Brazil. While poverty spreads like a plague, all I can do to take part in the struggle against the rich and powerful who so tarnish the image of our country is tell this little story.

I am reading a fine book on the Paris Commune, *Grande Histoire de la Commune*–five volumes that narrate the origins and issues of this movement, from Napoleon III to its spread through France like a great crusade. It reveals the French people's unceasing quest for liberty. The poor against the wealthy, centuries of struggle marked by blood, violence, and lack of understanding.

Reading these volumes reminds me of the 1935 uprising in Brazil, when, on an infinitely smaller scale than the Paris uprising but driven by the same aims and enthusiasm, a group of officers and civilians fought for liberty. For some reason I thought it might be useful to include a short text that I published in the *Jornal do Brasil*, protesting against the official version of the uprising that portrays it as a brutal and bloodthirsty adventure:

> For years many mistruths have been spread about the "intentona comunista," as they called this rebellion. The Communists did not slaughter troops in their beds because, obviously, troops do not sleep when they are on standby in their barracks.
>
> To get an idea of what really happened on that tragic night in 1935, one only has to read Hélio Silva, who quotes statements from Marshal Dutra and Captain Frederico Mindelo and extracts from the memoirs of Agildo Barata, Café Filho, and Luiz Vergara, etc. [129]
>
> I remember old friends who took part in the rebellion being dishonored by the monstrous distortion suggesting that they lacked principle and acted in a cowardly manner. In fact, the rebellion was all about enthusiasm and idealism.
>
> I recall our dear comrade Agildo Barata circulating around Rio de Janeiro, indifferent to the threats made against him and delivering, in our Copacabana office, an

account of what had really happened on that unforgettable night. He was perfectly calm, free from any hatred, all courage and determination.

But there was growing provocation, and with the help of the most reactionary individuals the idea spread throughout Brazil that there had been a bloodthirsty attempt to take power. As a result, an act of repudiation is held annually, but such commotion surrounds it that even the most liberal people in the government feel embarrassed to attend.

Nevertheless, political life in Brazil has made progress; censorship, violence, and authoritarianism are on the decline, so nothing justifies the extension of this long-established and regrettable farce.

Now back to my book on the Commune. It was Rimbaud who sung its praises: "*La promesse sonne, arrière ces superstitions, ces anciens corps, ces ménages et ses âges. C'est l'époque qui a sombré!*"[130] And the book concludes: "But the sacrifice has brought some men closer to the times of fraternity."

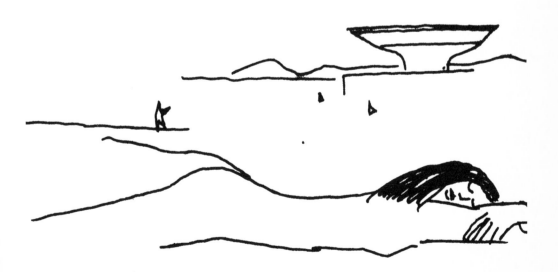

Today is a Sunday of rain and solitude. I am alone at the office, tired of life, of this obstacle course of tears and laughter.

An immense sadness overtakes me as I listen to a recording of old songs that evoke the passage of time, fears, growing old. There are elements of the past that I have never forgotten. Family, my beloved parents, friends who were so close. . . I cannot help crying, quietly, slowly, tenderly, with melancholy. I close my eyes and a strange serenity settles over me, as if I were off to meet them all again.

Then another song begins. It's old Ataulfo Alves singing some famous tune by Nelson Cavaquinho:[15] "Wipe that smile off of my road, I'm coming through with my sorrowful load."

What bothers me is not life's few rough edges, but the tremendous suffering of the destitute confronted with the indifferent smiles of the well-to-do.

At times during our extended car trips to Brasília, some small incident would remain impressed on our memory like something engraved there.

En route to the capital, until we reached the other side of the Petrópolis Mountains, the varied landscape was quite attractive. After that, however, the landscape became barren and nearly hostile, monotonous and tiresome. For miles and miles we crossed a region of sparse, stunted vegetation and scenery that spread out unchanged into the distance.

Halfway to Brasília, on the first curve of the highway just outside Juiz de Fora, we invariably spotted a gray-haired little old lady sitting on the front porch of her small house. Over time we grew accustomed to finding her there, watching peacefully and quietly as time raced before her sad eyes ever so mercilessly. For a few years she was always there at the end of the curve, as if waiting for us. After having seen her so frequently we wished to meet her, talk with her, listen to her stories, find out all about her life and her sorrows, and, who knows, even help her in some way. The little old lady seemed to sit there on the porch all the time, looking sad and obliging, watching the cars pass by. We wondered what kinds of worries she might have; whether her family gave her the loving care that people her age need, or whether she was weary and unhappy.

For years we focused our attention on the little old lady, until the day we rounded the curve to find a vacant front porch. Right then we realized that something was missing from the scenery–the very thing that lent it a more human and tender touch. We missed the little old lady and commented sadly on the life that had disappeared along with its joys and sorrows, helpless against a merciless destiny. We were faced with the drama of life, the end of the line.

For a while we speculated on the old woman's life. Perhaps she had once been pretty and had aroused passionate feelings, or she had been an unassuming homemaker devoted to her family, realizing sadly that her life was coming to an end. She may have suffered like a wilting flower losing its petals.

If she was religious, then she died peacefully, believing in the power and glory of the Lord. However, if she was not so optimistic, that is to say, if she took life as it comes–short, unfair, and inexplicable–her last days would have been even more dismal. Finally, after concluding that the latter assumption was the most probable, we drove on, discussing this indecipherable world in which our hopes and dreams dissolve into the precariousness of things and the certainty of nothingness.

It is on white paper that a boy amuses himself, on which he draws houses, trees, land and sea animals, the sun and the moon. He enjoys these magical moments in which beauty arises, pure and

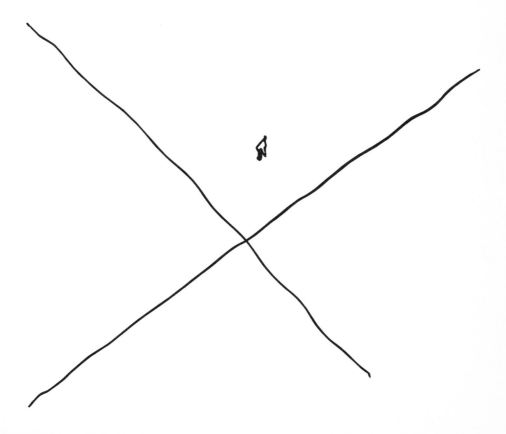

spontaneous, as it should always be. After that and throughout his lifetime, paper accompanies him in all his activities.

If he becomes a writer, it is on paper that he will write his novels and create his most remarkable characters and settings of drama or beauty. If he becomes an artist, it is on paper that he will sketch the masterpieces that will last throughout time. If he become a scientist, it is on paper that he will attempt to decipher the immense universe that surrounds us, to record distances, to ascertain new parameters, and to demonstrate our relative insignificance in comparison to the immensity of creation. Finally, if the boy grows up to become an architect, he will use paper and innovative techniques to design palaces, theaters, universities, and other shelters where human beings are born, grow old, and die.

Paper is the weapon of long-suffering people–those individuals who rise up against the injustice of life. Paper was present in the development of the applied sciences–from facsimile devices to state-of-the-art technology. And, oftentimes, it serves as a medium for bonding lovers, transmitting painful frustrations, and disseminating the worries and joys that destiny imposes on us.

It was on a sheet of white paper that Karl Marx announced a new world, which a privileged minority insists on postponing endlessly.

I was designing a hotel in Tel Aviv when I was asked to do a master plan for a small city in the middle of the desert. I was attracted to the project, since it was an unusual challenge. It called for a compact city to be built in a small area, but the city had to be expandable, so that new cities could be built over time and joined together to complete the project.

I was enthusiastic and began turning the idea over in my mind during my free time. I reviewed urban solutions from the past that had been modified gradually as human society progressed. I thought of the small medieval towns where everybody knew everybody else, where one could cross town on foot, effortlessly getting the exercise doctors recommend, walking to work, stores, and schools, all of which were close by. I was interested in how the inhabitants must have been happy to enjoy neighborly relationships, stopping to meet each other on the street; to enjoy community solidarity, the way life on this planet ought to be. They would have had a small square in the city where everyone got together. Life must have been more human in those times.

With the possibilities we have today, it should be easy to live the kind of life that I have always been attracted to—close to nature, free of the traffic problems that stifle our cities. I thought about a solution. First, I would have to build a few high-rise residential towers—fifty stories tall, regardless of the neighboring buildings. They would be distributed around the site in clusters, with suitable gaps between them. There would be fifty apartments with five hundred inhabitants per tower; the city would have one hundred thousand inhabitants.

Near the towers would be the necessary facilities: schools, daycare centers, athletic fields, small-scale retail facilities, and so on. Business and commercial areas would gradually emerge, as would the government agencies to manage the city. In the center of the city I would create a large square, site of the seats of government, administrative blocks, theaters, movies, and restaurants.

Divided into two sectors, the small city would allow vehicles only around the outskirts; in the city proper pedestrians would stroll through lush greenery, as in medieval towns. I could just see it, planted in the middle of the monumental desert like a small island, green and bustling. But I would have to foresee the city's future development to insure that it did not become unworthy of its origins, inhuman and polluted like all the world's major cities. I then created a highway system that anticipated the growth and multiplication of other small cities around and alongside mine, with areas for research, industry, and agriculture.

On re-reading this, I have a feeling that this idea was neither foolish nor impractical. It would neither be an unbearably dense and vertical city nor a horizontal one involving huge distances, but a small, human, and hospitable town of the kind now forgotten—except for the historical ones we love to visit. I liked Tel Aviv, mainly because it gave me the chance to see my old friend and colleague, David Resnick, a great architect. I was pleased to see that he lived happily there.

I was always something of a rebel. Having left behind all the old prejudices of my Catholic family, I saw the world as unjust and unacceptable. Poverty was spreading as if it was only natural and inescapable. I joined the Communist party and embraced the thinking of Marx, as I still do today. But life brings both joy and sorrow, and as unprotected citizens all we can do is move ahead, laughing and crying in this harsh world.

Perhaps that is why I have always accepted the moments of pleasure that life offers, feeling that we should live them fully, enjoying what beauty and love there is. This explains my contradictory writings, their mixed feelings of enthusiasm and anguish, as if two different people had been living my life. I recall that despite my constant pessimism, I have always shared fellowship with my companions.

Sometimes I like to think back to the good old days we spent at Clube dos Marimbás, chatting to friends on the beach at Copacabana in the shade of the old tropical almond trees. Borsói, Hélio, João Cavalcanti, Linhares, Silvio, Carlos Niemeyer, Gauss Estelita, and Braguinha[152] would come by and we would sit there until dusk, reluctant to leave. We talked about life, politics, soccer, girls, people we knew. The mood of friendship and good cheer repelled any possible negative feelings. Our families never came to the club. Mainly, it was a club for men who liked to share laughter, drink whiskey, and hang around, forgetting the world and its worries, idling the time away.

On Sundays, Borsói, who liked to cook, would say, "I'll fix lunch, but you'll have to listen to my speech." Laughing, he would then offer an inebriated ode to life, to the beauty of Copacabana, to "friends, women, and soccer." Chico Brito was a real wit. He often interrupted, forcing Borsói to stop his speech and reply amusedly, "Chico, go to whore's hell!" Then, being a polite person, he would add courteously, "Apologies to the ladies present."

The ladies in question were a few young women who often came to the club. They were cheerful and uninhibited, and they acted so naturally that under their apparently bohemian attitude they disguised optimum friendship and integrity. I remember how one evening Mário Catrambi was off to Brasília when he spotted one of the girls on the corner of Avenida Rio Branco. He pulled over and asked her to join him. She got into the car and off she went, with no suitcase and only the clothes she was wearing, to spend a week in the new capital.

Occasionally, the jokes went too far. I remember the night at the club when we laid out Chico Brito, who was completely drunk, on a table with a candle at each corner. It sure frightened the people who came in and took it for real! Ah, old Chico, how we miss you! He never worked a day. He spent his life at the beach, remarking to people he met there, as if he were at home, "It was so nice seeing you, come back again." Chico used to drift into my office almost every day, always smiling and in his bathing trunks. He failed to show up one day, and we soon heard the bad news: feeling ill, he had taken a sauna and then disappeared out on the ocean.

Every evening my cousin Carlos Niemeyer turns up at the office, soon to be followed by Rômulo, Renato Guimarães, Sabino Barroso, Fernando Balbi, and a few other, less steady visitors. Our discussion topic varies depending on what is happening in the country. Sometimes politics dominates, and then, since none of us thinks alike, the conversation heats up. Moments later, however, we are all friends again, ready to stroll off arm-in-arm. We often talk of the past, reliving our nighttime forays into Night and Day or Sacha's. We even relive our experiences abroad, such as the evening of the bullfight in Madrid when Hemingway crashed Rômulo's box, attracted by the lively goings-on there.

Yes, life can be tough, but some of us do have fun!

It was in March 1998 that I most regretted not having cut back sooner on my expenditures, which could cause problems for me overnight, as my friends had warned (and as I myself have commented in this book).

I had assumed personal and family commitments in times of plenty, but our expenses multiplied rapidly, and what I had been warned of came to pass. My daughter Anna Maria was assigned to control family expenses. She was shocked when she saw the numbers and said, "Dad, just stop helping everybody!"

What could I do? It was an uncontrollable urge for me. When I gave Luís Carlos Prestes an apartment, I wanted to eliminate the possibility that he might have housing problems, since he had nothing to fall back on. When I gave my driver a house. . . well it's all water under the bridge now. With this attitude toward life, I find it hard to adopt the logical, realistic position that others quite rightly defend.

I surely will build a home for my granddaughter, build an extension to my employee Aurélio's apartment, do complimentary design work for the Museum of the Arts of Brasília and for the monuments in memory of Carlos Drummond, Luís Carlos Prestes, and Darcy Ribeiro. I shall continue, whenever I can, to help others as much as possible.

I take great pleasure in giving to someone who asks for help. If I give so much that the person is astonished, I feel even happier. While strolling with friends, we frequently come across a homeless person or a beggar in the street, and I will give him or her the equivalent of five or ten dollars. Someone then says, "How silly. It's of no use at all." But it is an unexpected burst of happiness for the needy individual and for a fleeting moment, his or her life seems much better. I know four or five beggars who, over time, seem to have become my buddies. Two of them are in a wheelchair, and when they spot my car, they wave in greeting, happy to see me.

Brasília, with the white dome and block of the National Congress complex visible in the background

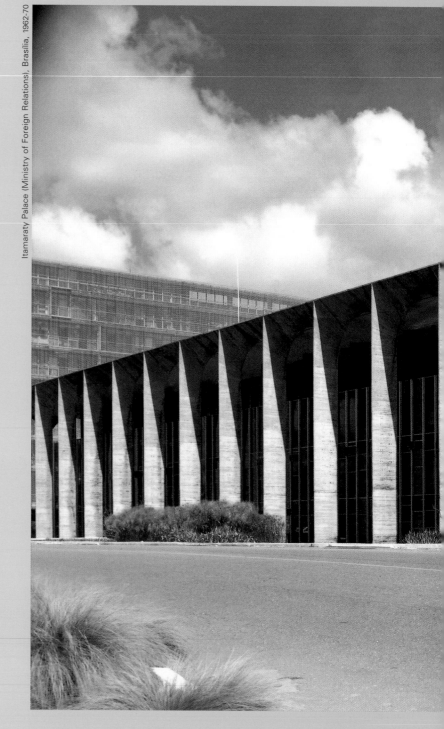

Itamaraty Palace (Ministry of Foreign Relations), Brasília, 1962-70

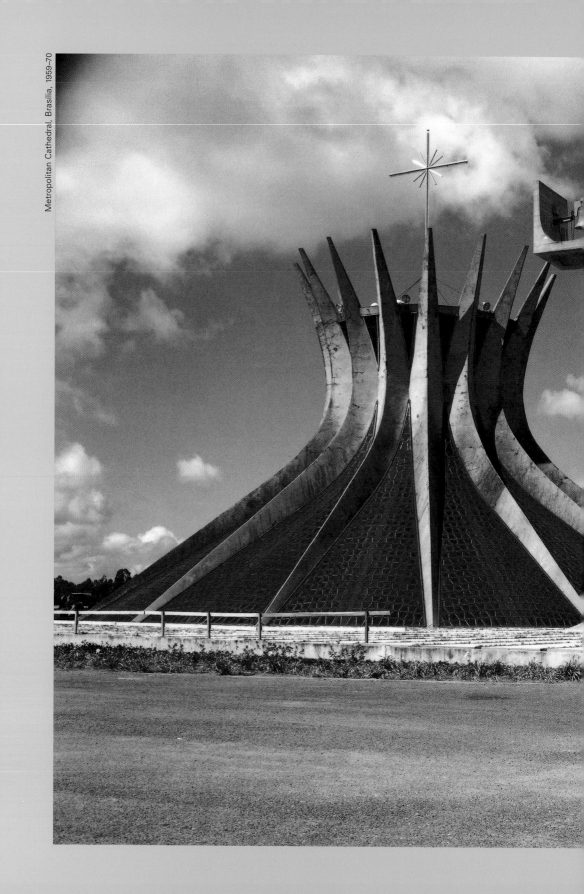

Metropolitan Cathedral, Brasilia, 1959–70

Casino, Pampulha, 1942 (shown after its conversion to a museum)

I remember a day in Algeria when I had received a considerable payment. The guard of the government-owned house where I lived ran up to speak to me, and I immediately realized that something had happened. I had helped him out several times, and even paid for his dentures, for which he seemed to thank me every day by smiling broadly to show his new teeth. That day he was crying and said he had lost his job and had to move far away from Algiers with his family. I gave him all I had in my pocket, glad to see him so astonished, as if a miracle had occurred.

I have often felt, in this way, that someone deserved my help. This was the case with my comrade Trifino Correa,[135] as I shall now explain. For years Trifino had been an inseparable friend and aide of Luís Carlos Prestes. I remember the day he sought my help. "I am desperate, Niemeyer," he said. "I've lost my daughter and I don't know what I am going to do. I decided to ask you. You are the only person who will not let me down. I need four hundred cruzeiros a month, for several months." I helped him out. Several months later I received this note from him; it shows such integrity that it is worth reproducing here:

"I have had a raise in my Army pension, so I would like to reduce the amount you give me to two hundred cruzeiros instead of four hundred, which I consider to be a large amount. Therefore, instead of coming every month to pick up the two hundred, which I know is a nuisance for you, I suggest picking up four hundred every other month. The next time will be in March. As soon as possible, I will be able to manage without the two hundred. Gratefully, Trifino Correa."

I never worry about being thanked for helping someone out, but it was a pleasure to help a comrade like him!

I often have the desire to write about this feeling, and I am proud to be this way. The rich should be reminded that fellowship is one of the few things that gives meaning to our wretched lives, that money is no guide to a person's worth, that we are all equally fragile and insignificant–rich and poor alike–when confronting this unjust world. Sharing is the most beautiful word there is, and to keep this precept close to one's heart is what God would want us to do, if He existed.

I do not know where I read this–maybe I did not, maybe it is my own idea: A woman is the physical and spiritual complement to a man. Without her, without her seductive charm and good company, man loses his capacity to dream and fantasize, which justifies and gives meaning to our lives.

I recall how, in my youth, women exerted great power over us men. Even after I was married, it was not easy to ignore that irresistible attraction that men feel for women throughout their lives. I have always loved my wife. She is beautiful, uncomplicated, and devoted to our family, as befits her Italian origins. I have always respected these qualities in her, and have therefore felt painfully guilty on certain occasions. I shall not justify this occasional guilt by blaming my persona, my genetic double, who is nastier than I am; though genetics obviously does have a lot to do with my permanent attraction to the female sex. I always tried to avoid parallel love affairs, but life seems to set us up. You suddenly find yourself inevitably trapped, often as a result of some problem, even a physical one. In reality this type of problem stems more from Mother Nature than from man, because, after all, this is the way she made us.

I shall say very little about my architecture here, since I have said practically all there is to say elsewhere. Neither do I wish to talk about the old rationalists. Today we enjoy total plastic freedom. Reinforced concrete has made new and unpredictable forms possible, beginning with Pampulha in the 1940s. We are living in a period of particular artistic creativity in architecture, a period marked by the search for beauty, invention, and fantasy, for architecture seen as true art.

I do not disregard the past. The individuals who built the pyramids, or the enormous vaults, or the old cathedrals, were truly great! I do not see the watershed as being between ancient and modern architecture, but rather, as Alvar Aalto says, between good and bad architecture. My architecture is very personal, and it should not be viewed as a new school to be followed. What is essential is that each architect make his own architecture. I know the enthusiasm we feel for a desired solution, and the hope with which we conclude a design. And that has to be respected. I do not criticize my colleagues.

In the past, I often clashed with those who rejected my ideas as an architect. Not anymore. After all, they are defending what they have achieved over the years as good professionals. Time goes by, and I welcome all kinds of architecture. There are always signs of talent and good architectural work in all of them, including those that are not my favorite style. I do not believe in socialist architecture in a capitalist country. It tends to be paternalistic; or worse, it perversely intends to mitigate struggles around old, hard-fought-for demands.

I do not know why I have always designed large public buildings. But, because these buildings do not always serve the functions of social justice, I try to make them beautiful and spectacular so that the poor can stop to look at them, and be touched and enthused. As an architect, that is all I can do.

My architectural oeuvre began with Pampulha, which I designed in sensual and unexpected curves. This was the beginning of the plastic freedom that reinforced concrete unleashed. Then came Brasília, where I glorified structure, inserting architectural style into it. By the time the structure was finished, architecture and structure were there as two things that must be born together and that together enrich each other.

When the military dictatorship was established, I was forced to move abroad. In foreign countries, I wanted to expose not only my architecture, but also Brazil's advances in engineering. In partnership with my engineer colleagues I filled spaces, reduced struts, and broke records to show the world that we in Latin America, a continent so exploited, were also capable of doing fine work.

My architecture became known and was executed everywhere: France, Italy, Algeria, Great Britain, Portugal, and even Saudi Arabia. Of course, this was something to be proud of after having spent most of my life bent over a drawing board. But if I were asked what, of all these projects, has given me the most pleasure, I would say it was to have taken the time to think about life in this unjust world that we must one day transform.

I have always confronted life as an unwavering rebel. After reading Sartre, I viewed life as an unfair and unrelenting tragedy. When I was a young man of only fifteen, I was anguished to think of man's destiny, doomed as we are to total abandonment, and defenseless against it. I was frightened by the idea of someday disappearing forever. Like everyone else, I have tried to erase such thoughts and instead take advantage of the pleasures of this brief and joyful passage on earth that fate grants us without our consultation. I have felt the ecstasy of the fantastic natural world around us, and, arm-in-arm with my friends, I cast aside the disturbing thoughts that so afflicted me when I was alone. I wore a mask of youthful optimism and contagious good humor. I was known as a high-spirited and spontaneous personality, a lover of the bohemian life-style, while deep inside I nursed a tremendous sorrow when I thought about humanity and life.

In my moments of solitude, I anxiously pondered this mysterious universe around us and recalled old Paul Gauguin, who wrote on one of his paintings so long ago, "Where do we come from, who are we, where are we going?" I resented the terrible injustice that exists in the world, which separates people from one another and devaluates certain social groups. I became a Communist, and I have spoken out against poverty all my life.

At times, I have felt that I was not wholly in agreement with my good comrades. For example, I have never believed that we should be optimists, that we should forget the drama of human existence, and that what is important to us is not death but rather the perpetuation of the species. These arguments did not persuade me, and I figured that the moments of anxiety that troubled me would also trouble our children. I responded by quoting Antonio Gramsci,[134] who once wrote in his prison cell in Italy, "Optimism is often the wish to do nothing and accept all."

I based my ideas on Sartre's existentialism and on scientific progress, convinced that everything is precarious, a truth that ought to prevail. Some claimed that this attitude represented the age of nihilism, the end of the great fantasies and grand conquests that had

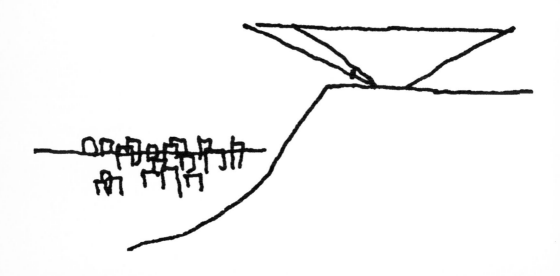

given man hope. I responded by going back to Sartre, who at the same time he declared all existence to be a failure, was defending Cuba and all oppressed peoples, telling his friends how he liked having money in his pocket so he could give it away.

I believed, as I still do, in Marx's doctrine, and I optimistically awaited the better world that we looked forward to. For years I was a loyal member of the Communist Party, passionately involved in the political struggle, a supporter of the October Revolution, of Lenin, Stalin, Mao, Prestes, Fidel, and everyone who rose up to fight for justice among men.

The years went by. I witnessed the Soviet crisis and the collapse of the Communist world, but I remained unchanged, convinced that what had happened could somehow be explained, something that the old Soviet Communists would be able to clarify. I was mystified; I felt that my political position was not consistent with the events taking place in Brazil and in the world. Many people accepted the Communist defeat as a consequence of old and irreparable mistakes, and quite a few others took it calmly, since it was what they had wanted all along. I refused to adopt those attitudes. I began to see the Soviet crisis as a natural phase of the political struggle, since humanity still had not reached the level that a Communist society, united in solidarity, demanded. I took refuge in the idea that the October Revolution, which had transformed the Soviet Union from a country of backward peasants into the second-greatest world super-power, had produced extraordinary progress. And that was quite enough for me.

I believed that our first step should be to transform humanity, making us simpler, more human, capable of understanding. In the words of Teilhard de Chardin, "being is more important than having."[155] Of course, I did not criticize Lenin. The October Revolution was an essential first step–the sign that the world would change, that the subsequent collapse of the Soviet regime was an accident on the road to the future, that Marx's ideals remain unchanged, and that the struggle was more conscious and more determined than ever.

I have never been against any public display of protest. It is imperative to protest. A word of protest, spoken with courage at the right time, has great merit. Often, when poverty is overwhelming and individuals continue to ignore it, the solution is to react. I think of my old Communist Party companions killed in political uprisings, murdered in reactionary torture chambers. I think of the heroic struggle of Cuba and of Fidel, leader of this suffering and exploited Latin America, and of how Latin America has become more vulnerable since Moscow is out of the picture.

The day Man understands that he is part of Nature, brother to the insects of the earth, the birds in the sky, and the fish in the sea, is the day he will understand his own insignificance and become simpler, more realistic, more human, and more sympathetic.

Within my limitations as a simple architect, I feel sad about Brazil's current situation, about the tremendous poverty run rampant and the bourgeoisie who scornfully cultivate even more destitution. I see the need for radical action. "We need to start the country with a clean slate," as Darcy Ribeiro would say. And this is a task that falls to the common people and their organized forces.

As I mentioned before, death was a constant concern of mine, and the idea that our bodies would simply disappear troubled me. As a child, I imagined with great sadness that one day suddenly I would no longer see my parents and brothers, or the mountains, rivers, and seas of my country. Over time, those thoughts have returned with increasing frequency during moments of solitude. That is why meeting my friends daily, laughing a bit with them, banishing those fears, has become indispensable to my inner balance. And that is why I avoid the solitude that older people like me often face.

So that is how I go on living, taking advantage of the moments of happiness that fate offers us on this inevitable march toward the great unknown. The certainty that we are Nature's children only deepens my despair. I am gradually trying to believe in the old adage that what counts is not age, but physical condition. I no longer have the same enthusiasm for going downtown with friends. Now we simply meet at the office, savoring our old stories, our old fun and games, and the dreams of our youth.

What is essential is that we remain true to ourselves, firm in our convictions, whether we chat about politics and soccer or about our meager lives in this fantastic universe, which, as we know, was not made specially for us, tiny beings that we are in the face of its immense grandeur.

I sometimes turn back to the distant past, now so remote, when we were still possessed with the urge to lead bohemian lives. I recall our old companions, the Café Lamas, the pool tables, Lapa, the bar on Rua Conde Lages, the man with the mandolin. . .

More flashbacks from the past: getting married, the Fine Arts school, my calling as an architect, living a more settled and contented life. And our office in the Porto Alegre building, the Café Vermelhinho, and the Clube dos Marimbás where, under the tropical almond trees, gazing out to the ocean at Copacabana, we talked of old times.

I thought of all this on that night. The meeting with my friends had ended early, so I was home beside Annita, watching her favorite soap opera on TV. I looked at her tenderly. How pretty she was! She sat with her chin resting on her right hand as always, smiling at the events taking place on the screen or frowning apprehensively at the world's evils. I recalled our wedding sixty years ago, then the birth of our dear daughter Anna Maria, and Annita tending our home. The happy moments we shared came to mind, the trips to different parts of the world: Paris, New York, Lisbon, Madrid, Buenos Aires, and Moscow. I could see her back on the Piazza San Marco in Venice, laughing happily at the pigeons perched on her shoulders; or in New York, where we spent long summer months and stretched out on the lawn in Central Park while our little Anna Maria chased squirrels.

When the television episode ended, Annita got up. "Oscarzinho, I'm off to bed. Don't forget to turn off the light."

I look at the room packed with family photos. I have to carefully move them aside if I want to get a book off the shelves. The hallway walls are also covered with large and small photos of our family. Touched by Annita's evident devotion, I go to the window and look out. Night has settled. Each apartment across the way harbors fortuitous joy. . . or infinite sorrow.

Although originally this book was not meant to dwell on an explanation of my architecture, it now becomes clear that to a large extent this is what I have to provide. After all, I have devoted nearly my entire life to this occupation. It has been my hobby and one of my greatest joys to devise new and creative forms suggested by reinforced concrete. I have sought to discover them, multiply them, and combine them with state-of-the-art technology to achieve an architectural spectacle.

In my lectures I have always emphasized that I do not consider architecture terribly important, and there is no contempt in my words. I compare architecture to other things that are more connected to life and Man; meaning the political struggle, the personal contribution that each of us owes to society, particularly to our less fortunate brothers. What can compare to the struggle for a better and classless world where all individuals are equal? In spite of this opinion, architecture has kept me very busy, leading me, as I do now, to defend my works and my point of view as an architect, and to debate architectural issues with a passion that life, so fragile and insignificant, seemingly does not justify.

I have always argued for my favorite architecture: beautiful, light, varied, imaginative, and awe-inspiring. These are words that, much to my delight, I found later in a Baudelaire poem: *"L'inattendu, l'irrégularité, la surprise et l'étonnement sont une partie essentielle et une caractéristique de la beauté."*[156]

I will not delve into details here, however; I will merely present my career as an architect, my doubts, my rebellion, my professional courage to do only what pleases and moves me–fearlessly and with no regard to preestablished rules. I divide my architecture into five stages: Pampulha, from Pampulha to Brasília, Brasília, my international experience, and finally, the later designs. I have never commented on how these different stages were influenced by what was happening in the architectural world and by my own thinking as an architect. Nor have I discussed the reactions that my work provoked, or my way of counteracting. Now, as I go over my designs, I better understand why an invariable trace of protest suffuses all the stages of my work.

On several occasions I have mentioned genetic information and how, in my opinion, it accounts for our qualities and defects, thus influencing our reactions. I shouldn't complain about this hidden being within us that genetic information creates and which so often dominates us. I have already mentioned how this "double" controls me when I begin a new design, taking me by the arm and leading me in trance along the pathways of fantasy to the new, unexpected shapes that are responsible for this architectural spectacle.

Neither should I complain about how this persona shares my enthusiasms and acts of resistance in this lifelong dialogue, interfering with my reactions and my work, informing the latter with my feelings, making my architecture the receptacle of either my interest or my contempt and protest. Thus, if you examine my architectural work in its different stages you will see how this old alter-ego has always acted, transforming these phases into sighs of relief in view of the blunders that, in my opinion, have affected architecture.

It all started when I began the Pampulha studies–my first phase– in which I deliberately disregarded the celebrated right angle and rationalist architecture designed with ruler and square to boldly

enter the world of curves and straight lines offered by reinforced concrete. On paper, while drafting these plans, I protested against such monotonous and repetitive architecture, which was so easy to create that it quickly spread from the United States to Japan.

I made this first move with the unexpected boldness that my persona demanded, covering the Pampulha church and the marquee of the Caso do Baile with varied curves. This deliberate protest arose from the environment in which I lived, with its white beaches, its huge mountains, its old baroque churches, and its beautiful suntanned women. Some individuals, who were still bound by the functionalist limitations of the time, tried to criticize the Pampulha complex, but it was so appropriate that, years later, in Paris, my French colleague De Roche stated: "Pampulha was the greatest thrill of my generation." It was the world of new shapes contraposed to an erroneous architecture on the wane.

From Pampulha to Brasília, my work followed the same trajectory of plastic freedom and architectural inventiveness, and I became aware of the convention of defending it against the limitations of constructive logic. Thus, if I designed a different shape, I had to have arguments to explain it. Every time I designed a curved block standing alone on a site, for instance, I presented it with accompanying sketches showing that the existing curved topography itself had suggested it. When I designed inclined facades, I likewise explained that these were intended to provide greater solar protection or exposure; when I designed an auditorium shaped like an ink blotter, I was addressing the problem of interior visibility; when I created a strut system in the form of an open fan, reducing the number of struts on the ground floor and increasing them on the upper floors, I cited economic reasons; when I proposed curved roofs with inclined supports at the edges, my justification was related to the structural problem of thrust; when I proposed a solution that combined curves and straight lines, I deferred to differences in ceiling height. In this way I defended my architecture and my fantasies, creating new forms and architectural elements that over time were added to the plastic vocabulary of our architecture, which was often used by my colleagues but not always at the correct scale and with the desired accuracy. I carried on like this for many years, always searching for a different shape and then explaining it afterward, as required.

During this period I took three trips abroad: the first one, at Lúcio Costa's invitation, to join him in the design of the Brazilian Pavilion for the 1939 New York World's Fair; the second to Venezuela, where, inspired by the local topography, I designed a museum in the form of an inverted pyramid; and the third to New York again, where I won by unanimous vote a private competition for the design of the United Nations headquarters.

I must confess that when I started my work in Brasília I was already weary of providing so many explanations. I knew that I was experienced enough to be rid of such justifications, and I could not care less about the inevitable criticism my designs were sure to raise.

As with the Pampulha phase, a feeling of protest possessed me in Brasília. It was no longer the imposition of the right angle that angered me, but the obsessive concern for architectural purity and structural logic, the systematic campaign against the free and creative forms that attracted me and which were viewed contemptuously as gratuitous and unnecessary. People talked about "purism"–about the "machine for living in," "less is more," "functionalism," and so on–without understanding that all this would be derailed by the plastic freedom made possible by reinforced concrete. Contemporary architecture was vanishing through its repetitive glass boxes.

I once imagined that the followers of contemporary architecture, grown tired of so much repetition, would someday become disappointed with the dogmas they once fiercely advocated and choose something different, finally assured that invention must prevail. This is occurring now, but once again they are making a mistake by tacitly following the adventure of postmodernism, reproducing the same building designs but adding anachronistic and outdated architectural details. This is the same "gratuitousness" they once criticized and have now admitted in its most simplistic form.

I sadly remember how, when a structural framework was completed, the architectural form necessary to finish the building was often still indefinite; nothing was known about it except that it would come later, as a secondary consideration. This was the result of imposing an erroneous technical rigor that purist designers, with their mediocre structures, had always accepted. In my opinion, it was up to architects to anticipate structural problems, so that by combining their imagination with technical sophistication they could create an architectural spectacle responsive to current trains of thought.

I decided to follow this line of thinking for the palaces of Brasília. They would be characterized by their own innovative structural form. As a result, minor details typical of rationalist architecture would recede against the dominant presence of the new structures. Anyone who observes the National Congress complex and the palaces of Brasília immediately realizes that once their structural framework was built, the architectural design was already in place.

I sought to experiment with reinforced concrete, primarily with the supports that tapered to very slender ends, so thin that the palaces seemed to barely touch the ground. I remember my great pleasure at designing the columns of the presidential residence, the Alvorada Palace, and my delight at seeing my idea reproduced everywhere. The columns were an architectural surprise that contrasted with the otherwise monotonous prevailing style. With the same keen dedication I worked on the design of the presidential office building, the Planalto Palace; and the Federal Supreme Court building at Praça dos Três Poderes. I pulled the columns away from the facade and stood before the blueprint trying to picture myself strolling amid them, trying to determine the different angles they would produce. This exercise prompted me to reject the simple, functional strut required for the structure and instead give deliberate preference to the newly designed shape. All along I laughed with my double about the "mistake" that, hopefully, the prevailing mediocre critics were

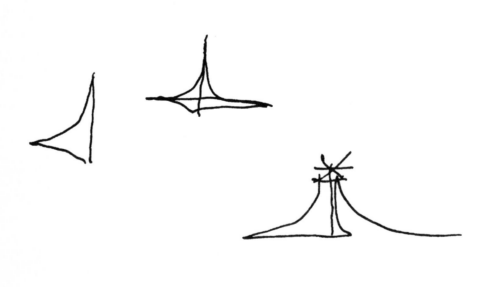

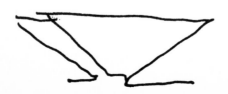

soon to discover. Nothing stopped them, however, and they were not curious. If they had been curious, if only they had read a little more–for example, these words by Heidegger–it would have done them some good: "Reason is the enemy of the imagination."[157]

One day, sitting in front of the Doges Palace, completely in awe of its admirable lightness, I found in that magnificent work by Calendario the example of what my architecture represented. And right there and then I wrote this brief text, imagining myself in dialogue with a rationalist architect. It was a simple, Socratic dialogue that I wish to reproduce here:

"What do you think of this palace?"

"Magnificent!"

"And what about its carved columns?"

"Very beautiful!"

"But you, a functionalist, would still prefer them to be simpler and more functional?"

"That's correct."

"But if they were, there wouldn't be this splendid contrast between the columns, full of arabesques, and the straight wall that supports them."

"That's true."

"So you must agree that when a shape creates beauty, its own justification lies in its beauty."

My designs for Brasilia have continued to pour forth. The theater, for instance, was conceived in three days over carnival.

I never complained. If there was no time to think, there was also no time to make undesired alterations. The search for an unusual solution fascinated me. In the Metropolitan Cathedral at Brasília, for example, I avoided conventional solutions, which had produced the old dark cathedrals reminding us of sin. On the contrary, I designed a dark entrance hall leading to the nave, which is brightly lit, colorful, its beautiful, transparent stained-glass windows facing infinite space. I always received understanding and support from the clergy, even from the Papal nuncio, who could not contain his enthusiasm upon visiting the cathedral: "This architect must be a saint; only a saint could devise such splendid connection between the nave, heaven, and God."

I designed the remaining buildings with the same degree of architectural innovation. In the National Congress complex, the dome and the saucer-shaped building were hierarchically arranged;

in the Ministry of Justice building, water spouted from the glass facade, like a miracle; and the Pantheon enhanced the Praça dos Três Poderes like a white bird. Only in the Ministry of Foreign Relations building did I do something different, eager to show how easily we could please everybody with a proper, generous but prosaic solution that required no sense and sensibility.

Now when I visit Brasilia I feel that our effort was not in vain; that Brasilia marked a heroic period of labor and optimism; that my architectural design duly reflects my state of mind and my courage to expose that which touched me most deeply. In my design I honored the volumes and free spaces of Lúcio Costa's master plan, its extraordinarily well-conceived characteristics that produced a monumental and hospitable city.

During the twenty years in which a military dictatorship ruled our country no one was particularly concerned with criticizing Brasilia, though permanent carelessness and contempt led to some parts of the city being considerably downgraded. I refer mainly to the subsequent construction of mediocre buildings that destroyed the city's intended urban unity. I had no alternative but to move abroad. Foreign countries are home to some of the best projects I have designed, namely the French Communist Party headquarters; Bobigny's Bourse de Travail building; the Cultural Center of Le Havre; the FATA Office Building in Turin; the Mondadori headquarters in Milan; and the universities of Constantine and Algiers, in Algeria.

During this phase, my fourth, the prevailing idea was to manifest not only the plastic freedom of my architecture but also the advancements in engineering in Brazil. I searched carefully for the solutions that each project demanded, eager to clearly define the parameters of my work as an architect. In the French Communist Party headquarters, I demonstrated the importance of maintaining harmony between volumes and free spaces on the exterior, which explains why the great workers' hall is located underground. In the Bourse de Travail in Bobigny, I showed a way in which it is possible to make economical architecture. There I economized in the main block but enhanced it with the free shapes of the auditorium. In the Cultural Center of Le Havre, I positioned the square below street level to shield it from the cold and from constant winds. This solution has no equivalent in Europe, as it created soft, almost abstract curves on the exterior walls. According to Massimo Gennari, this work received the following unexpected compliment from Bruno Zevi, at the Cairo

Congress: "I rank the Le Havre square among the ten best works of contemporary architecture."[138] At the FATA Office Building, I suspended the five floors from roof beams, an interesting structural solution that Massino Morandi, who designed it, described as follows: "For the first time I had the opportunity to demonstrate what I know about reinforced concrete." At the Mondadori headquarters, I designed the arches at varying widths to produce the unique, almost musical rhythm that characterizes the building. In Algiers, the grand free spaces, the fifty-meter free spans and the twenty-five-meter cantilevers create such powerful architecture that construction defects that resulted from the use of unskilled labor go unnoticed.

Now, in São Paulo, at the Memorial da América Latina, my design radically follows advanced construction techniques. There are no minor details, only seventy- to ninety-meter beams and curved shells. These form the great free spaces recalled by the project's theme. The memorial is a work whose monumental size corresponds to the greatness of its objective: to unite the people of an oppressed and exploited Latin American continent.

I have worked on very few projects of a social-welfare nature, and I confess that when I have done so, I always had the feeling that I was conspiring with the demagogic and paternalistic objectives such projects represent: to mislead the working class, which demands

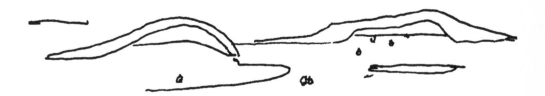

better wages and equal opportunities. I always rejected this mistaken, mediocre idea of an architecture that is somehow "simpler, closer to the people." When we built the CIEPs, we were happy to see that poor children liked them, as if the buildings gave the kids hope of some day having access to what only the rich enjoy today. As I see it, this idea of architectural simplicity is sheer demagogy, unacceptable discrimination, and at times it shows a reluctance to create that can only be explained by lack of talent.

On the other hand, monumentality never frightened me when a stronger topic justified it. After all, what remains in architecture are the monumental works, the ones that mark history and technical evolution – those that, socially justified or not, still touch us. This is beauty imposing itself on man's sensibility.

Oh! How great were the old masters, those who designed enormous domes, extraordinary vaults, ancient cathedrals!

Here, then, is what I wanted to tell you of my architecture. I created it with courage and idealism, but also with an awareness of the fact that what is important is life, friends and attempting to make this unjust world a better place in which to live.

1 Rodrigo Melo Franco de Andrade. Brazilian critic, art historian, and writer, he founded the National Historical and Artistic Heritage Service (SPHAN), later renamed the National Historical and Artistic Heritage Institute (IPHAN), of which he was first director.

2 Epitácio Lindolfo da Silva Pessoa. President of Brazil, 1919–22.

3 Tristão de Athayde, nom de plume of Alceu Amoroso Lima. Brazilian lawyer, journalist, and Catholic thinker, he chaired Centro Dom Vital, a civil organization linked to the Roman Catholic Church, and was a member of the Brazilian Academy of Letters.

4 Manuel Maria Barbosa du Bocage (1765–1805). Portuguese poet known as a libertine in the bohemian circles of Lisbon. He was arrested by the Inquisition in 1797 and imprisoned. His collected poems were published as *Rimas* in 1791.

5 Luís Carlos Prestes. Former Brazilian army captain who was an active participant in the 1935 Communist uprising, and a Federal District senator, 1946–48. During the military dictatorship in Brazil, which began in 1964, Prestes went into exile in Moscow. Following the general amnesty of 1979, he returned to Brazil. He died in 1990.

6 "To sail is a necessity. To live is not a necessity..." Line from a poem by Portuguese poet **Fernando Pessoa** (1888–1935).

7 Gauss Estelita. Architect. **Rômulo Dantas**. Real estate entrepreneur.

8 Renato Guimarães. Journalist and militant member of the Brazilian Communist party, where he befriended Niemeyer. **Sabino Barroso**. Architect who worked with Niemeyer in Brasília. **Ivan Alves**. Journalist who met Niemeyer in Paris. He became president of the Brazilian Press Association (ABI). **Fernando Balbi**. Engineer and businessman. **Carlos Nova de Niemeyer**. Filmmaker and founder of an important television production company.

9 João Aires Saldanha. Sports journalist and member of the Brazilian Communist Party. **Glauco Campelo**. Architect who worked with Niemeyer in the construction of both Brasília and the Mondadori headquarters in Milan. **Hermano Montenegro**. Architect who collaborated with Niemeyer in Algeria and Brasília.

10 Nightclubs in Rio de Janeiro.

11 Roberto de Oliveira Campos. Brazilian economist, diplomat, and politician, he was the first minister of economics and planning of the military dictatorship, 1964–67.

12 Laurinha Tinguassu. Owner of a famous brothel in Lapa, a district in Rio de Janeiro where intellectuals and bohemians gathered in the 1930s.

13 Antônio Jacobina. Engineer and Brazilian swimming champion. **João Brandão**. Bank executive and director of Banco Boavista. **Horácio de Carvalho Júnior**. Journalist, owner of the newspaper *Diário Carioca*. **Sílvio Cavalcanti**. Notary public in Rio de Janeiro. **Alfredo and Casimiro Rodrigues**. Merchants. **Tico Liberal**. Journalist for the newspaper *Diário Carioca*. **Oyama Rios**. Owner of a pharmaceutical business.

14 Tom Mix and **William S. Hart**. American heroes of early Hollywood adventure and cowboy movies, they starred in dozens of films from the 'teens through the 1920s.

15 Hélio Laje Uchôa Cavalcanti. Architect who collaborated with Niemeyer on the design of the National Aeronautic Center and Housing Complex in São José dos Campos, and the Ibirapuera Park complex in São Paulo. **Milton Roberto**. Architect, partner in the M.M.M. Roberto architecture firm, which designed the Brazilian Press Association (ABI) and Souza Cruz Company buildings in Rio de Janeiro. **José Reis**. Architect who worked at Lúcio Costa's office with Niemeyer. **Paulo Cabral da Rocha Werneck**. Self-taught draftsman and painter who worked at the architecture firms M.M.M. Roberto and Oscar Niemeyer.

16 Don João VI (1767–1826). King of the United Kingdom of Portugal, Brazil, and the Algarve. When Portugal was invaded by Napoleon Bonaparte in 1807, the king fled to Brazil with his family. In 1815, he proclaimed the Portuguese colony of Brazil an empire. He was crowned Prince Regent of Portugal in Brazil in 1818. The Imperial

Academy of Fine Arts, the Royal Library, the Royal Press, and the Botanical Gardens were created in Rio de Janeiro during his tenure.

17 Darcy Ribeiro. Brazilian anthropologist, politician, and intellectual who founded the University of Brasília. He held high political offices until the military dictatorship forced him into exile. After the general amnesty of 1979, he returned to Brazil where he became vice-governor and later senator of the state of Rio de Janeiro.

18 CIEP: Centro Integrado de Educação Pública (Integrated Center of Public Education). Designed by Niemeyer beginning in 1982, these innovative schools were conceived by Rio de Janeiro governor Leonel Brizola (see note 20) and Darcy Ribeiro (see note 17) to address the problem of public education in Brazil. The schools are open throughout the day, with full student access to facilities, meals, and recreation.

19 José Carlos Sussekind. Engineer and a principal associate of Niemeyer beginning in 1980.

20 Leonel de Moura Brizola. Prominent Brazilian politician until the coup of 1964, when he was persecuted and went into exile in Uruguay. Returning to Brazil after the general amnesty of 1979, he founded the Democratic Labor Party and became governor of Rio de Janeiro (1983–87 and 1991–94).

21 Jack Lang. French politician, French minister of culture, 1981–86 and 1988–91.

22 Carlos Bittencourt. Architect, member of the team that built Brasília. As a student he befriended Niemeyer at the National School of Fine Arts. **João Cavalcanti**. Architect. As a student he befriended Niemeyer at the National School of Fine Arts. **Fernando Saturnino de Brito**. Architect who worked at Niemeyer's Rio de Janeiro office.

23 Lúcio Costa. Architect and urban planner who is considered the father of Brazilian modernism. He designed the master plan for both Brasília and the district of Barra da Tijuca in Rio de Janeiro. Costa also headed the team that designed the Ministry of Education and Health building (Palácio Gustavo Capanema) in Rio de Janeiro, among many other projects. **Carlos**

Azevedo Leão. Architect, draftsman, and painter, he was member of the team that designed the Ministry of Education and Health building in Rio de Janeiro.

24 Jorge Machado Moreira. Architect and member of the team that designed the Ministry of Education and Health building in Rio de Janeiro.

25 Israel Pinheiro da Silva. President of Companhia Urbanizadora da Nova Capital (Novacap), the governmental building authority in Brasília, he became the first mayor of the new capital in 1960, and later governor of the state of Minas Gerais, 1966–71.

26 Gustavo Capanema Filho. Minister of education and health under president Getúlio Vargas, 1934–45, he was an important contributor to the cultural institutions of Brazil.

27 Carlos Drummond de Andrade. Brazilian poet who belonged to the so-called Minas Gerais school of Brazilian modernists who published the cultural magazine *A Revista*. **Manuel Carneiro de Souza Bandeira Filho**. Renowned Brazilian poet. **Abgard de Castro Araújo Renault**. Brazilian writer, member of the Brazilian Academy of Letters. **Afonso Arinos de Melo Franco**. Brazilian writer and politician, member of the Brazilian Academy of Letters. **Prudente de Morais Neto**, known as Pedro. Journalist and president of the Brazilian Press Association (ABI), 1975–77. **Mário Raul de Morais Andrade**. Brazilian writer who organized the 1922 Modern Art Week in São Paulo, which promoted cultural nationalism.

28 Cândido Torquato Portinari. Painter, draftsman, and printer. **Jacques Lipchitz** (Chaim Jaboc Lipchitz). Renowned Russian-born French sculptor who moved to New York in the 1940s. **Celso Antônio de Meneses**. Brazilian sculptor who studied in Paris with Bourdelle. His sculpture *Moça reclinada* (Reclining woman) is installed in the gardens of the Palácio Gustavo Capanema in Rio de Janeiro. **Bruno Giorgi**. Brazilian sculptor whose monumental works *Monumento à juventude* (Monument to Youth), and *Guerreiros* (Warriors) are installed in the gardens of the Palácio

Gustavo Capanema in Rio de Janeiro, and the Praça dos Três Poderes in Brasília.

29 Advisors in the office of Gustavo Capanema, minister of education and health.

30 Novacap. Companhia Urbanizadora da Nova Capital.

31 Emílio Garrastazu Médici. Third president of Brazil (1969–74) during the military dictatorship that began after the coup of 1964.

32 Afonso Eduardo Reidy. Architect who was associated with the design of the master plan for Rio de Janeiro in 1929.

33 Marcus Vinícius Cruz de Moraes. Brazilian diplomat, poet, and composer. **Carlos Echenique**. Salesman. **Luiz Jardim**. Writer. **Eça**. Nickname of **Walter Garcia Lopes**, renowned tramp of the Lapa district, who befriended artists and intellectuals. **Galdino Duprat da Costa Lima**. Architect who had monarchist ideas and Communist friends.

34 Madureira is a neighborhood in Rio de Janeiro renowned for its bohemians and the unconventional lifestyle of its residents.

35 Juscelino Kubitschek de Oliveira. President of Brazil from 1956 to 1961, he was renowned for his ambitious public works. He commissioned the construction of the new capital, Brasília.

36 Agildo da Gama Barata Ribeiro. Militant member of the Brazilian Communist Party.

37 Francisco de Assis Chateaubriand Bandeira de Melo. Brazilian journalist, politician, and diplomat, he owned the news broadcast conglomerate Diários Associados.

38 Lelé. Nickname of **João Filgueiras Lima**, an architect who was a close friend of Niemeyer and member of his team in Brasília.

39 Gastão Luís Cruls. Brazilian writer who directed the literary review *Boletim de Ariel*. **Pedro da Silva Nava**. Brazilian physician and writer known as a memorialist.

40 Aleijadinho (1730s–1814). Prolific Brazilian sculptor and architect, renowned for his rococo statues and religious imagery, which was opposed to the sobriety of his churches.

41 Diogo do Couto (1542–1616). Portuguese historian who wrote the last chapters of the *Décadas da Asia*, one of the first

great accounts of European overseas exploration and colonization by João de Barros. **Fernão Lopes** (c. 1389–c. 1460). Portuguese historian and first royal chronicler, he was a key figure in medieval historiography.

42 António Vieira (1608–1697). Portuguese Jesuit missionary, writer, orator, and diplomat, he played an active role in Portuguese and Brazilian history. His famous sermons exhorting the various races in Brazil to join the Portuguese colonizers in arms are considered the first expression of the Brazilian national mystique of forming a new mixed race. **Alexandre Herculano de Carvalho e Araújo** (1810–1877). Portuguese historian, novelist, and poet, he was a prestigious advocate of liberal opinion. He is credited with introducing romanticism to Portugal. **José Maria de Eça de Queiroz** (1845–1900). Portuguese writer committed to social reform, he introduced naturalism and realism to Portugal. He is considered one of the greatest Portuguese novelists. **Joaquim Maria Machado de Assis** (1839–1908). Brazilian poet and writer, he is considered the classic master of Brazilian literature. He had little interest in contemporary political and social issues; instead, his novels reflect his aristocratic, cosmopolitan cynicism and the urban lifestyle in Rio de Janeiro.

43 Max Jacob. French poet who belonged to the circle of Cubist painters and Surrealist writers in Montmartre, Paris, at the beginning of the twentieth century; he influenced the new directions of modern poetry. **Jacques Monod**. French biochemist who was awarded the 1965 Nobel Prize in Medicine for his work on the genetic regulation of cell metabolism.

44 Celso Ferreira da Cunha. Brazilian philologist and professor of Portuguese.

45 Jorge Leal Amado de Faria, known as **Jorge Amado**. Renowned twentieth-century Brazilian novelist and militant Communist. **Ferreira Gullar**, nom de plume of José Ribamar Ferreira. Contemporary Brazilian writer, poet, and art critic.

46 Alberto Moravia, nom de plume of Alberto Pincherle. Italian journalist, short-story writer, novelist, and key figure in twentieth-century Italian letters.

47 Ricardo Jaimes Freyre. Bolivian poet and teacher.

48 Gasogene. An apparatus used for burning charcoal to produce gas fuel for powering internal-combustion engines.

49 Silioma Seltzer. Architect who contributed to Niemeyer's projects in São Paulo.

50 Getúlio Dornelles Vargas. Leader of the 1930 rebellion that put an end to the "coffee-elite," or powerful landowners' hold on the government, he became president of Brazil in 1930. He implemented a policy of administrative centralization, economic nationalism, and social reforms that helped to modernize the country. Although his first tenure, 1930–45, evolved into a virtual dictatorship, he is revered by his followers as the "Father of the Poor" for his battle against big-business and the landed gentry.

51 Otavio Frias de Oliveira. Entrepreneur and owner of the Folha da Manhã newspaper conglomerate.

52 José Lopes. Portuguese architect and life-long associate of Niemeyer, with whom he collaborated on projects in Brasília, Algeria, and Europe.

53 Diógenes Arruda Câmara. Brazilian Communist Party leader and underground activist during the military dictatorship.

54 Antônio Benedito Valadares Ribeiro. Governor, congressional representative, and later senator for the state of Minas Gerais.

55 Nápole. Italian owner of a marble store in Rio de Janeiro that supplied material for Niemeyer's construction projects.

56 Milton Soares Campos. Brazilian politician from the state of Minas Gerais, he was minister of justice in 1964–65.

57 Marco Paulo Rabello. Engineer for the Pampulha complex in Belo Horizonte and several buildings in Brasília designed by Niemeyer.

58 "*Le Corbusier, après avoir longtemps illustré la discipline puriste et la loyauté de l'angle droit, ayant senti dans le vent les prémices d'un nouveau baroque venu d'ailleurs, semble avoir décidé d'abandonner l'honnête angle droit, sur lequel il avait cependant tendance à se croire des droits particuliers. Au fond, le baroque-né se fait justice a lui-même, et comme toujours avec un immense talent.*" **Amédée Ozenfant**. French painter and theoretician who, with Le Corbusier, founded the art movement known as Purism.

59 Joaquim Maria Moreira Cardozo. Architect, engineer, and poet who worked with Niemeyer, notably on the construction of Brasília.

60 Niemeyer refers to Parque da Gamaleira, an exhibition building in Belo Horizonte that he designed in 1968; the structural engineer was Joaquim Cardozo. During construction, in February 1971, part of the Gamaleira building crumbled, killing 65 people. The project was abandoned, and Cardozo, a respected engineer, was unfairly blamed for the accident, which ruined his career.

61 Júlio Niskier. Hydraulic engineer who worked on several projects by Niemeyer.

62 "*Il faut faire chanter les points d'appui.*" **Auguste Perret**. Belgian-born architect who worked primarily in France during the first half of the twentieth century. He is known for his contribution to the vocabulary of reinforced-concrete construction.

63 Oscar Nitzke. Swiss architect who worked with Le Corbusier in Paris in the 1920s, and later at Wallace Harrison's firm in New York during the design of the United Nations headquarters (1947–50).

64 Budiansky. Engineer and one of Le Corbusier's associates.

65 Max Abramovitz. Architect and partner at Wallace Harrison's firm (Harrison, Fouilhoux, and Abramovitz), which designed the United Nations headquarters.

66 Milton Prates. Brazilian Air Force pilot assigned to the construction team for Juscelino Kubitschek's residence in Brasília.

67 Catetinho. Diminutive form of Catete, the presidential residence in the former Brazilian capital, Rio de Janeiro.

68 In 1957, when Niemeyer began work on Brasília, 19 cruzeiros was equivalent to US$1. Thus forty thousand cruzeiros equaled roughly US$2,100. The value of the cruzeiro fluctuated dramatically during the twentieth century; in 1967, when Niemeyer designed the Rio de Janeiro airport, the "nóvo," or new, cruzeiro was the official currency, and NCr3.20 equaled US$1 (see p. 86)

69 *Cavaquinho*: Small, four-stringed instrument similar to a banjo.

70 César Prates. Owner of a notary public and friend of Juscelino Kubitschek. **Rochinha**. Freeloader who lived off the good grace of others in Brasília. **Juca Chaves**. Builder who also owned Juca's Bar in Rio de Janeiro. In Brasília, he directed the construction of Catetinho, the presidential residence. **Bené Nunes**. Pianist and conductor. **Dilermano Reis**. Guitarist who composed great Brazilian hits.

71 Tibério César Gadelha. Journalist who worked for Niemeyer before establishing his own public-works construction company.

72 Succesors to Juscelino Kubitschek, their badly-administered presidencies paved the way for the military coup of 1964. **Jânio da Silva Quadros**. Colorful and at times eccentric populist, he unexpectedly resigned the presidency after seven months in office (Jan.–Aug. 1961). **João Belchior Marques Goulart**, known as **Jango**. Leftist politician, he advocated a protective, nationalist economic policy and land-redistribution program during his presidency, 1961–64. He was deposed by the military coup.

73 Marcos Jaymovitch. Architect who worked with Niemeyer in Brasília and became Niemeyer's secretary in exile, in Europe and Algeria.

74 Ivan de Souza Mendes. Army general and temporary governor of the Federal District of Rio de Janeiro, he was appointed by the dictator-president Humber to Castelo Branco in 1964.

75 Colonel Manso Neto. One of the principal advisers to General Emílio Garrastazzu Médici, who at the time was president of Brazil. The episode narrated here took place in 1971.

76 Mário Catrambi. Physician and jujitsu wrestler who hung out with Niemeyer's bohemian group at Clube dos Marimbás.

77 Sir William Halford. British architect and member of the international jury that selected the master plan for Brasília.

78 Di Cavalcanti. Painter and caricaturist, he was one of the organizers of the 1922 Modern Art Week in São Paulo. His work focused predominantly on Brazilian themes featuring the female figure. **Ari Evangelista**

Barroso. Composer of Brazilian popular music and author of numerous hits.

79 André Sive. French professor of urban planning and member of the international jury that selected the master plan for Brasília.

80 Heron de Alencar. Language teacher at the University of Brasília, he went into exile in Paris, where he collaborated with Niemeyer on the design for the University of Constantine in Algeria.

81 Miguel Arraes de Alencar. Brazilian politician who was forced into exile after the military coup in 1964.

82 Luis Hildebrando Pereira da Silva. Scientist and researcher at the University of São Paulo who went into exile after the military coup in 1964. In Paris he directed a Pasteur Institute team of researchers seeking a vaccine for malaria. **Ubirajara Brito**. Scientist who went into exile after the military coup in 1964. In Europe he collaborated with Niemeyer on the design for the University of Constantine in Algeria. **Euvaldo Mattos**. Physician from Bahia who worked as an intern in Paris, where he befriended Niemeyer.

83 Evandro Cavalcanti Lins e Silva. Renowned Brazilian magistrate and journalist who was minister of foreign relations in 1963 and minister of the Federal Supreme Court, 1963–69.

84 Carlos Magalhães da Silveira. Architect who worked with Niemeyer and married his daughter, Anna Maria.

85 Amauri Kruel. Head of the military office of the presidency, 1961–62 and minister of war, 1962–63.

86 *negrinho*. Racist Portuguese term for a young black man. This derogatory term was commonly used to refer to blacks and mulattos in Brazil, and is revealing of the prejudice that permeated Brazilian society during the period Niemeyer describes in this book.

87 Humberto de Alencar Castelo Branco. First president of the military dictatorship in Brazil, 1964–67.

88 Astrojildo Pereira Duarte Silva. Founder of the Brazilian Communist Party, of which he was the first secretary general. He was arrested by the military dictatorship in October 1964.

89 Birunga. Nickname of architect **Oswaldo Cintra Carvalho**.

90 Maria Luíza de Carvalho. Director of *Módulo*. **Marcus Lontra**. Art critic, writer for *Módulo*. **Vera Lúcia Guimarães Cabreira**. Marketing and advertising associate at *Módulo*. After the publication was discontinued she worked as an associate in Niemeyer's firm.

91 Paul Nizan. Politically engaged, left-wing French writer, he was a member of the French Communist Party until 1931.

92 Charles Gosnat. French congressional representative and secretary of finance of the French Communist Party.

93 Raymond Aron. French sociologist, historian, and political commentator, contemporary of Jean-Paul Sartre. His work *L'Opium des intellectuels* (The Opium of the Intellectuals) (1955) criticizes left-wing conformism and the totalitarian tendencies of Marxist regimes.

94 Claude Leroy. French Communist Party leader and director of the Communist newspaper *L'Humanité*.

95 Jean Genet. French criminal and social outcast-turned-writer whose novels denounce social injustice. He became a pioneer of avant-garde theater, especially the Theater of the Absurd.

96 Dejelloul. Vice-president of Algeria. **Houari Boumedienne**. Algerian army officer and revolutionary of the National Liberation Front of Algeria, he became president of Algeria in 1965 after instigating a coup against President Ahmed Ben Bella.

97 Georges Marchais. Secretary general of the French Communist Party, 1972–94. **Jacques Tricot**. French engineer, builder, and PCF activist.

98 Jean Prouvé. French engineer and builder known for his contributions to the art and technology of prefabricated metal construction. He was responsible for the structural design of the French Communist Party building in Paris, designed by Niemeyer. **Jean de Roche**. French architect who collaborated with Niemeyer in Paris. **Paul Chemetov**. French architect who founded the Atelier of Urban Science and Architecture.

99 "Oscar, Marie is dead. A great sorrow."

100 Nauro Esteves. Architect who directed Niemeyer's office in Brasília.

101 Originally quoted in English. **Konrad Lorenz**. Austrian zoologist and the acknowledged founder of ethology, he won the 1973 Nobel Prize for Medicine.

102 Giorgio Mondadori. Italian publisher who commissioned Niemeyer with the design of the headquarters of his publishing company, Mondadori, in Milan. He published several books by Niemeyer and on Niemeyer's work.

103 Cecília Scharlach. Architect who collaborated with Niemeyer on several projects, including the Memorial da América Latina in São Paulo.

104 Lionello Puppi. Italian architecture history teacher and critic at the Univeristy of Padova, Italy, who wrote two books on Niemeyer's work.

105 Filippo Calendario. Italian architect and sculptor active in the first half of the fourteenth century. Among his major works is the Arsenale in Venice. The design of the Palace of the Doges, also in Venice, is in part attributed to him.

106 Jorge Vale. Architect who collaborated with Niemeyer on several projects, including in Algeria.

107 Edgard Graef. Brazilian architect who at the time taught at the University of Brasília. **Fernando Lopes Burmeister**. Brazilian architect who joined Niemeyer's Algerian team in the 1970s. **Fernando Andrade**, known to his friends as Capacete (Helmet). Architect who worked at Niemeyer's firm beginning in 1973, when he joined the team in Algeria.

108 Arakawa. Japanese-born architect who settled in São Paulo and joined Niemeyer's team in Algeria.

109 José Aparecido de Oliveira. Journalist and politician who was, at the time, congressional representative from Minas Gerais.

110 Araribóia (Vicious Snake). Morubixaba Indian who, in the mid-sixteenth century, helped Portuguese settlers expel the French who had founded a colony in the Guanabara Bay.

111 Lily de Carvalho Marinho. French-born wife of Horácio de Carvalho.

112 Jean Baptiste Debret. French painter who, in the early-nineteenth century, traveled to Brazil where he made portraits of the Brazilian imperial family.

113 Moacir Gomes de Souza. Engineer who directed the engineering department of Novacap, the governmental building authority in Brasília. **Peri Rocha France**. Engineer, director of Novacap.

114 Gilberto de Melo Freyre. Brazilian sociologist and politician. Among his renowned works is *Casa grande and senzala* (The Masters and the Slaves), an account of the relationship between Brazil's Portuguese colonizers and their African slaves.

115 Niemeyer refers to the so-called Coluna Prestes (Prestes Column), a famous two-and-a-half year, 15,000-mile protest march against the government by a group of some 1,500 troops led by Prestes, a captain in the army. Though the march failed to provoke real political change, it sparked popular support and became almost a mythologized event in Brazilian history.

116 Salomão Malina. Engineer and militant member of the Brazilian Communist Party; he was elected chairman in 1987. **Geraldão**. nickname of **Geraldo Rodrigues dos Santos**, a dockworkers' union leader and member of the PCB.

117 Nélson Werneck Sodré. Brazilian army officer and historian whose books are considered classics.

118 José Aparecido de Oliveira. Journalist and political figure. He served as Brazil's minister of culture in 1985 and governor of Brasília, 1985–88.

119 Barbara Hepworth. British abstract sculptor who befriended **Henry Moore** during their studies together. **Charles Despiau**. French sculptor who developed a sensitive, classical style akin to that of Aristide Maillol. **Aristide Maillol**. One of the most important sculptors of the twentieth century, he attempted to preserve and purify the tradition of classical Greek and Roman sculpture.

120 Honório Peçanha. Brazilian sculptor who created the statue of Juscelino Kubitschek for the JK Memorial.

121 Adolpho Bloch. Russian-born business-man and publisher of *Manchete*, he supported the construction of Brasília. **Aimé Lamaison**. Mayor of Brasília from 1979 to 1982.

122 Sarah Luísa Gomes de Lemos Kubitschek. Wife of Juscelino Kubitschek, she presided over the construction of the JK Memorial.

123 João Batista de Oliveira Figueiredo. President of Brazil, 1979–85.

124 Maria Amélia Melo. Architect who worked with Niemeyer on the Memorial da América Latina project in São Paulo and several plans for buildings in Minas Gerais and Brasília. **Hélio Penteado**. Architect who collaborated with Niemeyer on plans for the state of São Paulo. **Hélio Pasta**. Architect who worked with Niemeyer on several projects in São Paulo. **Paulo Mendes da Rocha**. Renowned Brazilian architect. **Ubirajara Giglioli**. Brazilian architect. **Massahi Ruy Ohtake**. Renowned Brazilian architect. **Eduardo Corona**. Architect who worked with Niemeyer at his Rio de Janeiro office. **Ciro Pirondi**. Architect and former president of the Brazilian Institute of Architects (IAB).

125 Jair Valera. Partner of Niemeyer's granddaughter, Ana Elisa, at the architectural firm that produces the blueprints for Niemeyer's projects.

126 Marianne Peretti. French painter and stained-glass window designer who settled in Brazil, where she designed the stained-glass windows of the Metropolitan Cathedral at Brasília. **Athos Bulcão**. Brazilian painter and draftsman who collaborated with Cândido Portinari and Niemeyer. **Firmino Saldanha**. Architect and abstract painter who designed the stained-glass window/mural at the Caixa Econômica Federal (Federal Savings and Loan Bank) building in Rio de Janeiro. **João Câmara Filho**. Draftsman, painter, and printer.

127 Franz Weissman. Austrian-born sculptor who settled in Brazil. **Alfredo Ceschiatti**. Brazilian sculptor whose works are in the collections of several Brazilian museums, and the Brazilian embassies in Moscow and Berlin. **Caribé**, nickname of **Hector Julio Paride Bernabó**. Argentine painter who moved to Brazil and settled in Bahia. **Poty**, nickname of **Napoleón Potyguara Lazzarotto**. Draftsman, printer, and illustrator who made the mural for the Acts Hall of the Memorial da América Latina in São Paulo. **Carlos Scliar**. Brazilian painter, draftsman, and printer. **Mário Gruber Correia, Luis Antonio Vallandro Keating**, and **Victor Arruda**. Brazilian painters. **Tomie Ohtake**. Japanese-born Brazilian painter and printer.

128 Niemeyer has misquoted Sartre's statement: *"Le monde peut fort bien se passer de la littérature. Mais il peut se passer de l'homme encore mieux."* "The world can well do without literature. But it can do even better without Man."

129 Hélio Ribeiro da Silva. Physician, journalist, and historian. **Eurico Gaspar Dutra**. Army officer and president of Brazil, 1946–51. **Frederico Mindelo**. Army officer who was promoted to Army general after he supported the military coup in 1964. **João Café Filho**. President of Brazil, 1954–55. **Luiz Vergara**. Brazilian journalist and advisor to president Getúlio Vargas, whom he accompanied until the end of his political career.

130 "The promise resounds, despite all these superstitions, these ancient bodies, these arrangements, and these ages. It is today's age that has gone under." **Arthur Rimbaud** (1854–1891). French poet and adventurer, renowned among the Symbolist movement, who markedly influenced modern poetry. In 1871 he was a volunteer in the forces of the Paris Commune.

131 Ataulfo Alves de Souza. Popular composer and singer from the 1940s. **Nelson Cavaquinho**. One of the most renowned composers of Brazilian popular music.

132 Borsói. Businessman in the printing industry. **Sílvio Niemeyer**. Brazilian architect and cousin of Oscar Niemeyer. **Braguinha**. Merchant.

133 André Trifino Correa. Militant Communist and army officer who took part in the 1930 revolution and the 1935 Communist uprising. He subsequently received a dishonorable discharge from the army, but was restored to the rank of captain in 1968.

134 Antonio Gramsci. Twentieth-century Italian intellectual and political theorist, he founded the Italian Communist Party. He spent the last eleven years of his life in prison; his writings *Lettere dal carcere* (Letters from Prison) were published posthumously in 1947.

135 Pierre Teilhard de Chardin. French Jesuit priest, philosopher, and paleontologist who was involved in the discovery of Peking Man in 1929. His writings were published postumously, as the Jesuit order banned them during his lifetime.

136 "The unexpected, irregularity, surprise, and awe are a characteristic and essential part of beauty."

137 Martin Heidegger. German philosopher who iscounted among the main exponents of twentieth-century Existentialism.

138 Bruno Zevi. Well-known twentieth-century Italian architecture critic.

Chronology

1900s

1907 Oscar Niemeyer is born in Rio de Janeiro.

1920s

1929–34 Bachelor's degree in architecture from National School of Fine Arts (ENBA) in Rio de Janeiro, where Lúcio Costa becomes director in 1931.

1930s

1930 *Revolution against the so-called "coffee presidents," the elite landowners, brings President Getúlio Vargas to power.*

1935 Begins work at Lúcio Costa's office.

1936 At Lúcio Costa's office, participates in the design of the Ministry of Education and Health building.

Meets Gustavo Capanema and Le Corbusier in Rio de Janeiro.

1937 *Vargas seizes absolute power and institutes a highly centralist administration known as Estada Nôvo (New State).*

Designs the Obra do Berço building in Rio de Janeiro.

1939 Goes to New York with the team that designed the Brazilian Pavilion at the World's Fair.

Receives the New York City Medal.

1940s

1940 Juscelino Kubitschek, mayor of Belo Horizonte, commissions Niemeyer to design the Pampulha complex.

1945 *Vargas is ousted by the military.*

Joins the Brazilian Communist Party.

1946 *A republican constitution is adopted in Brazil.*

Designs the Banco Boavista headquarters at Candelária in Rio de Janeiro.

1947 Goes to New York with the committee commissioned with the design of the UN headquarters. In the bid, his design is selected in first place.

1949 Awarded Honorary Membership in the American Academy of Arts and Sciences.

1950s

1954 Designs a building for the residential complex Hansaviertel in Berlin, for which 15 internationally renowned architects were commissioned. Travels to Germany, Poland, Czechoslovakia, and the Soviet Union.

Designs the Modern Art Museum in Caracas, Venezuela.

1955–61 *Juscelino Kubitschek is president of Brazil.*

1955 Founds the journal *Módulo* in Rio de Janeiro.

1956 Juscelino Kubitschek commissions Niemeyer to design the new capital of Brazil.

Appointed head of the architecture department of Novacap, the governmental building authority for Brasília.

Member of the jury to select the master plan for Brasília.

1957–60 Designs in Brasília, among other buildings, the presidential residence, Palácio da Alvorada (Palace of Dawn); the National Congress complex; the presidential office building, Palácio do Planalto (Palace of the Highlands); the Federal Supreme Court.

21 April 1960 *Brasília is dedicated as the official capital of Brazil.*

1962 Appointed coordinator of the School of Architecture at the University of Brasília.

Travels to Lebanon to design the permanent Rachid Karami International Fair in Tripoli, and a sports complex.

1963 Receives the International Lenin Prize.

Appointed honorary member of the American Institute of Architects (AIA).

1964 *Military coup deposes President João Goulart; beginning of military dictatorship in Brazil.*

Military dictatorship bans the publication of *Módulo.*

Appointed honorary member of the American Academy of Arts and Letters.

1965 Leaves University of Brasília in protest against the education policy imposed by the new regime.

Travels to Paris for the exhibition "Oscar Niemeyer—L'architecte de Brasília" at the Pavillon de Marsan.

Receives the Juliot-Curie Medal and the Grand Prix of Architecture and Art awarded by *L'Architecture d'aujourd'hui.*

Begins to design projects in Africa and Europe, including the headquarters of the French Communist Party in Paris.

1967 Unable to work in Brazil because of political pressure, he settles in Paris.

1968 Designs the Mondadori publishing house headquarters in Milan, Italy.

1969 Designs the University of Constantine in Algeria.

1970s

1971 Releases in France the prototype of an armchair, his first example of industrial design.

1972 Establishes his office on the Champs Elysées.

Designs the Bourse de Travail building in Bobigny and Le Havre Cultural Center.

1975 Designs the FATA Office Building in Turin, Italy.

Módulo resumes publication in Rio de Janeiro.

Decorated with the Order of Infante D. Henrique in Portugal.

1978 Founding member and first president of Centro Brazil Democrático—CEBRADE (Brazil Democratic Center).

1979 *General amnesty restores political rights in Brazil. Many exiled Brazilians return home.*

Decorated with the Légion d'Honneur in France.

Retrospective exhibition "Oscar Niemeyer, Architecte" opens at the Centre Georges Pompidou in Paris, and travels to Venice and Florence.

1980s

1982 Designs the Sambódromo used for samba parades during Carnival in Rio de Janeiro.

1983 Retrospective exhibition "From Aleijadinho to Niemeyer" opens at the Museu de Arte Moderna in Rio de Janeiro, and travels to the UN headquarters in New York and the Architecture Department of the Illinois Institute of Technology in Chicago.

Designs the Centros Integrados de Educação Pública—CIEPs (Integrated Centers of Public Education) with Darcy Ribeiro.

1985 *General elections end the military hold on the government.*

Resumes the design of projects for Brasília.

Decorated with the Grand Official Order of Rio Branco in Brazil.

1987 Designs the Memorial da América Latina in São Paulo, and the headquarters of the newspaper *L'Humanité* in France.

Exhibition "Oscar Niemeyer—Architetto" opens at Palazzo a Vela, in Turin, and travels to Bologna and Padua.

1988 *A democratic constitution is adopted in Brazil.*

Receives the Pritzker Prize for Architecture.

1989 Receives the Príncipe de Asturias Prize for the Arts awarded by the Fundación Principado de Asturias, Spain.

Appointed Honorary Member of the Royal Institute of British Architects (RIBA).

1990 Leaves the Brazilian Communist Party.

Receives the Medal for Merit awarded by the College of Architects of Catalonia, Barcelona.

Decorated Knight of the Order of St. Gregory the Great by the Vatican.

Exhibition "Óscar Niemeyer" opens at the Fundació Caixa de Barcelona, and travels to London and Turin.

1991 Designs the Museu de Arte Contemporânea of Niterói, Rio de Janeiro, and the Parlamento da América Latina in São Paulo.

Publishes *Conversa de arquiteto*.

Receives the Grã-Cruz Order of Rio Branco in Brazil.

1992 Publishes *Meu sósia e eu*.

1996 Designs the monument Eldorado-Memória, which he donates to the Movement of Landless Rural Workers.

Awarded the Golden Lion at the VI International Architecture Exhibition at the Venice Biennale.

1997 Preliminary sketches for the Caminho Niemeyer (Niemeyer's Way), Niterói, Rio de Janeiro; the Museu de Arte Moderna, Brasília; the headquarters of TECNET—Tecnologia; and the Americana City Hall in São Paulo, and the Riocentro Convention Center in Rio de Janeiro. Niemeyer's ninetieth birthday is commemorated with a series of exhibitions of his works throughout Brazil.

Publishes *Museu de Arte Contemporânea*.

1998 Receives the Royal Gold Medal awarded by the Royal Institute of British Architects (RIBA).

Preliminary sketches for the Santa Helena Cultural Center in Paraná; the Ulysses Guimarães Palace and Memorial in Rio Claro, São Paulo; the Guiomar Novaes Music School in São João da Boavista, São Paulo; the Darcy Ribeiro Memorial at the Rio de Janeiro Sambódromo; the Maria Aragão Memorial in São Luis, state of Maranhão; the Touros Landmark Monument and the permanent Nativity Scene, in Natal, state of Rio Grande do Norte.

1999 Designs, among other projects, a new theater for the Ibirapuera Park in São Paulo; the Cultural District in Brasília; the Administrative Center in Betim, Minas Gerais; the Commemorative Monument of the fifth Centennial of the Discovery of Brazil in São Vincente, São Paulo.

2000 Exhibition "Escultura de Oscar Niemeyer" at the Museu de Arte Contemporânea, Niterói, Rio de Janeiro.

Designs Módulo Educação Integrada (Integrated Education Unit) (MEI), daycare centers integrated within the CIEPs system.